WICKSY AND THE KING'S SHILLING

WICKSY AND THE KING'S SHILLING

PETER WICKS

ISIS
LARGE PRINT
Oxford

First published in Great Britain 2011
by ISIS Publishing Ltd.

Published in Large Print 2011 by ISIS Publishing Ltd.,
7 Centremead, Osney Mead, Oxford OX2 0ES
by arrangement with
The Author

British Library Cataloguing in Publication Data
Wicks, Peter, 1933–
    Wicksy and the king's shilling. - - (Reminiscence)
    1. Wicks, Peter, 1933 - - Childhood and youth.
    2. Great Britain. Army - - Military police - -
    Biography.
    3. Draftees - - Great Britain - - Biography.
    4. Large type books.
    I. Title II. Series
    355.2'2363'092–dc22

ISBN 978-0-7531-5273-7 (hb)
ISBN 978-0-7531-5274-4 (pb)

Printed and bound in Great Britain by
T. J. International Ltd., Padstow, Cornwall

The Send Off

By
Wilfred Owen

Down the close, darkening lanes they sang their way
To the siding shed,
And lined the train with faces grimly gay.

Their breasts were stuck all white with wreath
And spray
As men's are, dead.

Dull porters watched them, and a casual tramp
Stood staring hard,
Sorry to miss them from the upland camp.
Then, unmoved, signals nodded, and a lamp
Winked to the guard.

So secretly, like wrongs hushed up, they went,
They were not ours:
We never heard to which front these were sent.

Nor there if they yet mock what women meant
Who gave them flowers.

Shall they return to beatings of great bells
In wild trainloads?
A few, a few, too few for drums and yells,
May creep back, silent, to still vintage wells
Up half-known roads.

The Return

By
Peter Wicks

Back down the sunlit tracks they came that day,
To the siding shed
And stumbling, left the train, blind faces, shattered
grey.

Their heads were bandaged white, bemedalled, nay,
These were not dead!

Nurses led them and that same tramp
Stood staring hard.
Watched their return to the upland camp,
Now a haven and that tramp
Blinked, swallowed hard.

Now publicly, our wrongs redeemed, they went
Through dead strewn flowers.
We knew from which front this very few were sent.

Blind, still they yet mock what women meant
Who threw them flowers.

Should they return to beatings of wild bells?
This one trainload.
This broken few, too few for cheers and yells
Now led back silent from that muddied hell
Down longed for roads.

My father, Frank Wicks of Cowley, spent many months in the trenches of the First World War. He was fascinated by my stories of Germany, a country which he had never seen. I asked him what it had been like going to war. He was very reluctant to talk about it, but he did point me to the poems of Wilfred Owen. I was so impressed by his poem *The Send Off*, that I wrote a poem in his style and called it *The Return*.

Frank George Wicks of Cowley
1885–1953, died aged 67

DEDICATED TO:

My father, who inspired me.
My wife, Barbara, who encouraged me
to keep on writing.
Becky Curtis, Kirsty Small and Hannah Barney, of
ISIS, who also encouraged me and supported me.
Julia Buckle, who prepared the manuscripts.
Mike Thomas Palmer and John Colella, without
whose help I might not have finished this book.

The Journey

March had come in like a lamb and was now throwing its weight about in a very lion-like manner. Thursday in March 1950 was early closing day, which was a relief as we had already spent half the morning pushing the shop door shut against the wind, which swirled up and down the high street, blowing over rubbish bins and buffeting cyclists and buses alike. It bowled hats along the pavements, upended umbrellas and ladies skirts with equal abandon, and, every few minutes, it interspersed with flurries of soot pellets and white hailstones.

As it was early closing day, I had hoped to get a game with the Oxford Nomads Rugby Team that afternoon. The Nomads were a team made up of amateur rugby enthusiasts, who played in the Oxford Thursday League. They were mainly comprised of shop workers and college servants and anyone else whose half-day fell upon a Thursday. I knew that I was second reserve to play against the Culham Theological College, and the prospect of being trodden into the mud by this group of oversized, mayhem-loving, would-be bishops did much to diminish my enthusiasm. The prospect of playing in the biting wind, and the thought of having to cycle ten miles to the college, did not help, either.

It had been a slow morning with few customers to serve. Ralph Mander had been boring all the young apprentices, me included, with his reminiscences of being a wartime R.A.F. Policeman in Bermuda. Mr James, our dancing salesman, had been practising some new dance steps in the basement cabinet showroom with Elsie, our elderly invoice clerk, for a competition they were entering. Mr Ward, our buyer, was snoring behind a huge pile of invoices, which he was supposed to be filing, and Billy Kimber, our elderly carpet porter, was doing his stand-up cockney comic routine for the ladies of the counting house. Mr Allen, our Director, Neville Coobs, our Despatch Manager, Ray Smith and the van men were playing a makeshift game of darts in the lino cellar. Gordon Hastings of the carpet department and John Phillips of the adjoining linen department were playing a fierce game of chess on one of the glass-topped counters. Mr Mack, the linen buyer, and his assistant, Mr Hopkins, were conferring with a linen goods representative in his office, and David Rivers was chatting to his fiancée, whilst sitting upon the staircase of the soft furnishing department.

Mr Massey, the head porter and timekeeper, rang the bell for closing time, and seconds later, we were racing up to the head of the basement grand staircase to clock out. I knew that I did not have a lot of time, and so I dashed out into the inclement weather and down to the little warehouse in Bear Lane where the staff kept their bicycles. I had a lightweight, waterproof suit for cycling in which I kept in a small compact roll behind the saddle — a fat lot of good when the bicycle was 200 yards away, and it was raining as if it had just been invented.

I was already too wet to bother with the suit by the time I had reached my bike, so I leaped on and headed down towards The Plain and on to Rosehill.

I had bought new mudguards from Halfords on the corner of Long Wall Street, planning to replace the cracked and discoloured white plastic ones that I felt detracted from the appearance of my gleaming gold Hercules Kestrel racing bike. So, the night before (Wednesday), I had settled down to the task and had no sooner removed the old guards, than the heavens opened, and I was forced to retreat into the sanctuary of our warm kitchen, leaving the new, smart, white and gold Bluemel's deluxe mudguards on the kichen doorstep.

I had every intention of fitting them once the rain had stopped, but alas, I had not done so. I now regretted it as the front wheel spun a thin spray of slush up the front of my suit and into my face, whilst the rear wheel threw up another deluge of spray, which covered my back. And, of course, I didn't have my waterproofs on.

"Mum will sort it out!" I said to myself, in the manner of teenage sons everywhere. Yes, Mum would sort it out, and she did.

I reached Rosehill, still pedalling furiously, and there, bicycling along in front of me, was Mr Howse, our local insurance collector. The "green man" my dad always called him, whereupon my mother would sniff and declare that he was just jealous.

"Your father would not know a gentleman if he got up and hit him!" Mother would say, acidly. A confusing remark which always left me puzzled.

Mr Howse *was* a green man. His bicycle was a gold and green painted steed — what was called a deluxe sports model, twice the weight of mine, with enclosed chain case, deep mudguards, and with two headlamps and attached batteries case fixed to its crossbar. It had a kickstand similar to the ones fitted to motorbikes and a buffed brown leather briefcase carried in the front carrier basket next to the two-tone bell. Mr Howse himself was a small, neat-looking man, who always wore green, except for his highly-polished brown shoes and his black bowler hat. He could have been aged anywhere between forty and sixty, though I later discovered that he was in fact nearly eighty. The way he rode his bike always reminded me of a university Don or business executive at a desk — I cannot explain why. He looked like a gentleman; if he had been a street cleaner or a navvy, he would still have looked like a gentleman. The way he raised his hat to all and sundry, his manner of stepping aside to let old people pass, his carefully modulated voice and his pleasant face — it all gave the impression that he really cared about people, it came as no surprise to find out that he was a Methodist lay preacher.

Now, true to form, he was cycling determinedly up the hill, wearing green oilskins with a matching hood that was pulled down over his bowler hat and attached to his chin by a length of elastic. Every so often, the crosswind would catch him under his cape and send him flapping and careering towards the grass verge like a demented crow. Even so, he managed to touch his hood and hat in greeting as I struggled past.

I finally reached home, and what a sight met my eyes! There was my mother, standing on the dining table having hysterics. The cat had caught and delivered to the house a large brown rat, as a gift for her, and Mum, who had once panicked at the sight of a fur glove dropped carelessly on our sofa, was not appreciative. The rat was skidding and leaping dementedly around the room, with our cat in enthusiastic pursuit, emitting feline cries of what probably translated as "Tally Ho!".

Taking the situation in at a glance, I grabbed the broom and chased the rat out of the back door, falling over the cat and twisting my ankle in the process. Both rat and cat disappeared into my father's potato patch, and the coast was clear. My mother was not reassured, however and was adamant that she would not come down off the table until I'd proven that the rat really was gone. I stumbled around on one good leg, banging about under table, chairs, settee, cupboards and beds until she was persuaded that there were no further rodents in the house.

Satisfied, Mother began to descend; she teetered precariously as she attempted to climb down off the dining table and onto a chair, and I was called upon to assist her. Now mother was the first to admit that she was no lightweight, and I had already wrenched my ankle and was using the broom as a makeshift crutch.

To make matters worse, we had a linoleum floor, which was quite slippery when wet, and, of course, I had tramped in absolutely dripping. With my bad leg supported by the broom, I reached up to steady Mother down. She put her weight on my shoulder, and I, in turn, leaned more heavily on the broom . . . and the broom handle skidded across the lino. I was brought almost to my knees, and Mother, with one leg extended towards the dining-room chair, landed her foot heavily on the seat, all her weight bearing down on the medium heel of her court shoe, which cut straight through the somewhat flimsy three ply; she wound up with one leg extended on the table behind her and one leg trapped in the chair frame. She looked a little like a hurdler in a high-speed camera still — except this was not so funny. Clearly in pain, she was unable to move, and, strong though I was, I could do little to help on my own.

It was at this point that Mr Howse came up the garden path. Once a month he collected the insurance premiums along our road — I had forgotten that he was due today. My mother always had a cup of tea and a biscuit, together with the payment book and money, waiting on the front windowsill, where he preferred to stand so that he could chat to my parents for a few minutes before raising his hat and cycling off to his next port of call.

He now rapped on the window and, upon hearing my mother's cry of distress, together with my call for assistance, dashed around to the back door, let himself in and helped ease Mother off the table until she stood on both feet, though still with one leg securely trapped in the frame of the chair.

Mr Howse was an eminently practical man, so after I had got a flat blade screwdriver from my father's tool box, he tapped and lifted each tack in turn until he removed the plywood rectangle from the frame of the chair, then we sat mother at the table, with the plywood still round her leg. There was a large gap in the plywood around her knee, and splinters were threatening to scratch her skin. Mr Howse took two library books and wedged them either side of her knee with the spines of the books running parallel to the crack, then we both exerted pressure, folding the wood panel upwards until it split suddenly in two.

Mother's leg was unharmed, though a little uncomfortable, and she gratefully thanked Mr Howse, then bustled round her kitchen, producing a date and walnut cake (which I must have missed), as well as three great cups of tea.

Whilst the kettle was boiling, Mr Howse, who it turned out also taught first aid, checked my ankle and bandaged it with a support he kept in his briefcase for emergencies. Finally, when we were all settled with tea and cake, my mother asked, "Have you heard how the travellers are getting on?"

"One of our managers comes in from Wallingford, and he saw them being moved on by a police van outside 'Back Hand Mansion'. He couldn't see what happened, except for a brief glimpse, because at that point the bus carried on."

"I take it that C.J. was there, complaining as usual!" said mother, bitterly. She did not like C.J., but then few people did. My mother was a Labour Councillor, and she had often crossed swords with C.J., who was a man totally obsessed with money and power. He was always trying it on with the Council; one of his last stunts was to put a fence around several acres of Common Land and to have it patrolled by men with dogs. Having held the land for seven years and a day, he was able to register the land as his because of some old law.

He had once visited our school and given us a lecture on business practices. He described himself in glowing terms as a "highly successful business man". I wondered if he knew that most of south Oxfordshire referred to him as "Scrooge". He treated his tenants badly, and few stayed in his employ for long. The only remark my father made when I had described his somewhat boastful lecture was, "Nobody worships his creator as much as the self-made man!"

"He may have a lot of money," said my mother, "but otherwise his life is a mess. He's had two wives walk out on him, and I believe the third one is about to go the same way. He has no true friends, and his favourite saying has always been, 'Your best friend is your pocket'!"

This then was C.J. — a small, squat man, who habitually sat on a cushion to make himself appear taller. No one had ever seen him smile, and he had deep worry lines on his face, presumably caused by worrying about money and the acquisition of it.

"If he can't take it with him when he dies, I reckon he won't go!" said Dad, who rarely said a bad word about anybody.

8

"Back Hand Mansion" was the name given to his home by the locals. It was a large country house with an imposing drive facing onto the A40.

But what was this about travellers? What did they have to do with C.J.? Who were they and why did C.J. call the police? I had heard rumours at work of a strange couple slowly making their way along the London to Oxford road. According to eyewitnesses, this couple were progressing slowly, rarely covering a mile a day.

Had I been able to ride to the rugby match as intended, it seemed that I would have passed the couple coming the other way. But as it was, I couldn't, I didn't, and Mr Howse kindly offered to leave a message with our vicar, the Reverend Claude Buckwell, who would phone the Theological College on my behalf, though it transpired that the match was cancelled anyway due to flooding on the pitch.

With nothing else to do but sit and hold skeins of knitting wool for my mother to roll into balls, I pumped her for information regarding the travellers.

According to my mother, with her inside Council information, Oxfordshire and Berkshire social workers were very concerned about the strange couple, but they seemed to have declined all offers of help. It seemed that they were attempting to move all their worldly goods by hand. Having started off in the east end of London some months before, their party consisted of an enormous man, slightly older than me, a crossbreed Alsatian dog and an old and frail lady in an ancient wheelchair. They also had an old costermonger's wheelbarrow piled high with old pieces of furniture and carrier bags and half a dozen sacks and an old bicycle upon which the sacks were hung.

It seemed that the man would wheel his bicycle, complete with sacks, to a point several hundred yards on, deposit the sacks, then cycle back to the handcart. After roping the bicycle to his shoulders, he would push the handcart to the sacks. Meanwhile, the dog sat guarding the old lady. When the man had reached his drop-off point, he would whistle, and the dog would race down to take up station under the cart. The man then cycled back and, again roping the old bicycle to his shoulders, wheeled his mother slowly down to where their baggage lay. Both couple and dog were in a poor state. He was finding it difficult to walk and had rags tied under his shoes with baler twine, presumably to make the going softer.

When they stopped for the night, they pulled the handcart into the shelter of a friendly hedge, and stretched tarpaulin out across the wheelchair to make a temporary shelter for the night.

Quite a few people had tried to help, but they were mistrustful of everyone, and their dog was overprotective. Another problem was that neither spoke much English. He had a cleft palate, which made speech almost unrecognisable, and when she spoke, it was in a tongue that only he seemed to understand.

It was unfortunate that they chose to park up for the night opposite "Back Hand Mansion". Unfortunate, too, was the fact that when C.J. rose that morning, having looked out of his bedroom window over his purloined acres, the first thing he saw was the humble little shelter set up on the pristine grass verge fronting his property, and, insult of all insults, their tarpaulin was tied to his elegant railings. Almost apoplectic with fury, he had dashed out in his dressing gown, in spite of the rain, to confront the couple.

It appeared that the dog had been hunting during the night, for there on the grass were two rabbit skins and an appetising stew was heating up on a little wood fire. According to one of the servants, who had no love for him, C.J. kicked the stew over and tried to rip the tarpaulin off, exposing the travellers to the driving rain.

At this point, the dog went for him, and he claimed that he had been badly bitten by the animal. Doris, the servant girl, maintained that the dog did nothing of the sort, and certainly there were no marks to prove such a thing had happened.

In due course, having been called by C.J., the police appeared, and, having taken statements from C.J. and Doris, the police took the dog away in their van, and the couple were forced to move on in the driving rain, minus their protector.

That morning, C.J. dismissed Doris without notice for disloyalty.

"There was no way I was going to carry on working for a lying creep like him, especially when he couldn't keep his hands to himself! It was just that he got in first."

I got home late on Friday night because I had had to travel by bus (my ankle was still playing me up). There, waiting for me on the dining-room table, was a buff-coloured envelope — my first O.H.M.S. communication. I was to be called up for National Service. This meant I would have to take time off from work and report to a set of offices in New Inn Hall Street in the centre of Oxford city, there to attend a medical to make sure that I was fit enough to join the army.

The following Monday saw me hobbling up a steep rickety staircase and into a very large room, which presumably had been some sort of old warehouse. The building was so old and decrepit, that it seemed in imminent danger of collapse.

"Pray that the woodworm don't stop holding hands!" said one wag. "Otherwise the building will collapse, and then we are all in trouble."

There must have been fifty or so lads of my age gathered around the floor in small groups when a very small man in uniform came into the room carrying an enormous megaphone. He could not have been over 4' 6" tall. I well remember that he had enormous black shiny boots.

"Look at the size of those feet!" said the wag. "He wouldn't need to shoot the enemy; he could trample them to death! What's more, all those medals! If he had any more, he would have to wear them on his back!"

It was true; he wore so many campaign ribbons on his diminutive jacket, that there hardly seemed room for pockets.

The soldier with the megaphone now addressed us. He had an unusually deep voice, and it seemed to vibrate up from his boots.

"Those aren't boots!" said the comedian. "They're echo chambers!"

"Right gentlemen!" he roared. "I am going to call out your name, and as I call them out, you will answer, "Here Staff!" and then form a line in the middle of the hall."

He duly called out our names, and then a young, and very pretty, Royal Army Medical Corps nurse walked down the line and handed each of us a sheaf of papers, a paper sack and two small bottles. Just as we were casting around to ask one another what we should do, there was a clatter on the stairs. The door burst open, and in tumbled my old friend John "Ginger" Thorne.

"Brandy!" he croaked. "Give me brandy! These stairs are a killer. No one told me that I had to climb a parachute jump."

Then he saw me, and a broad grin lit up his freckled face.

"Well, if it isn't my old mate, Wicksy. What are you doing old chap?"

"Same as you by the looks of it," I responded.

"What did you do to your foot?" he asked. I told him. "With a bit of luck you could dodge this. Me, I've got too much to do to get called up. As far as I am concerned, it's a bloody waste of time."

"Mind your language!" said the pretty young nurse, severely.

"Don't tell me you haven't heard worse than that before," John replied in a loud voice. "I'll wager that you yourself have used far worse. I've been out with a lot of nurses in my time, and what they get up to is no one's business."

"That's nice for you," she replied sweetly. "And when you grow up, perhaps your mother will let you come out by yourself!"

There was such a roar of laughter from her audience that the tiny staff sergeant came out to see what all the laughter was about. Was Ginger discomfited?

"Not a bit chap," he said with a broad grin, blowing her an elaborate kiss. "I think I am in love!" Turning to me he asked, "How did you get here?"

"By bus," I replied. "How did you?"

"By military policeman!" he answered, grinning. "The army has been after me for weeks. I wanted to come, but I kept forgetting the dates. But these two Redcaps turned up at our ma's, and now here I am."

I walked across and peered out of the grubby window down to the street. Sure enough, there were two large military policemen sitting in their jeep, puffing away on two small cigars.

"Play your cards right, and I'll get you a lift," said Ginger, unabashed as usual. The rest of the room was looking at him with unconcealed respect. "It's a waste of time anyway; there is no way I could get through a medical. My doctor reckons that I am a mystery of medical science; it's a wonder I'm alive. You name it, I have it!" I looked at him — five foot eight of muscular body, so ginger you could almost light a fire off him and glowing with health, he looked the fittest person in the room.

Now, we were all instructed to strip off to our underpants, putting our clothes into the sacks provided for that purpose. For some minutes we stood, a shivering shambling line, unable to look one another in the face, dejected and miserable whilst, from a room next door, came the sounds of hearty laughter and the unmistakeable chink of crockery.

Eventually, after what seemed like an eternity, the army doctors trooped in, each attended by a uniformed nurse, and took up positions at desks placed at intervals around the room. Then it started.

One by one we filed round, going from one desk to another in turn. We were prodded, poked and, in one embarrassing moment, ordered to cough whilst being tested for a rupture.

Ginger, it has to be said, looked positively ill; he swayed at one time, had a glass of water brought for him and complained plaintively. I realised that he was making a serious attempt to fail the medical. He was so convincing that I almost believed it myself. He took twice as long as everyone else — and then came his master stroke! He began to foam at the mouth. We were alarmed — the nurses clustered around him, and then he was rushed into the other room. He returned looking pale and shaken just as we were putting our clothes back on.

"What happened?" I asked

"The crafty bleeders only put a stomach pump on me!" he answered, bitterly. "Where is the trust I should like to know."

15

At that moment, the staff sergeant called us to attention, and, one by one, we learned the results of our examination. With one exception, we had all been graded A1, whilst Ginger had been graded A2. In other words, we were all fit for military service. Ginger was appalled.

"What if I had been passed A3?" he demanded.

"You would have been dead!" came the smug reply. "We gave you A2 status because we believe that you have a mental problem."

I duly got my lift home in the military police jeep. This was quite strange really, because six months later, I became a military policeman.

Just as we were leaving, the staff sergeant crooked a finger at Ginger. "A word to the wise, son," he said. "Next time you try the old froth in the mouth trick, try Pears soap — it doesn't taste so good, but you get more convincing bubbles."

Miss Franklin had a pony cart. She was a familiar figure on our estate of Rosehill and also in the neighbouring villages of Cowley, Littlemore, Iffley, Sandford and Botley. She was a source of admiration to many and an equal source of irritation to others, for she was what is now called a Jehovah's Witness. Several times a week, in fair weather and in foul, she would crank up the large gramophone she carried on the seat beside her and play Bible tracts and talks which were delivered in strong mid-west American accents by the individual commentators.

She had trained as a nurse and was always to be found where the sick and destitute needed her the most. She and her sister owned a large farm by the Oxford-Henley Road, just outside Sandford upon Thames. Their father, who at a very young age had won the Military Cross in the Flanders trenches during the First World War, had registered himself as a conscientious objector after he had become a Jehovah's Witness in the 1930s. He had been thrown into prison for his beliefs, where he had died, a victim of prison abuse and pneumonia, only to be followed several weeks later by his wife, who died of a broken heart. So it was that in 1943, the girls had found themselves running a large modern farm, with a great deal of success.

Because the farm had been deemed to be of national importance to the food industry, the girls had had half a dozen Italian prisoners of war billeted with them to provide labour, together with a retired farm manager to advise them. Such was the level of expertise shown, that by the end of the war, they owned the adjoining farm as well. Both farms each had a set of fine labourer's cottages, and these were now occupied by groups of Italian families in such happy profusion, that the locals renamed the area "Little Tuscany".

Harry Smith had arrived at the farms the year before — a real mystery figure. No one seemed to know much about him, and if the Misses Franklin knew anything, they kept it to themselves.

Curiously enough, no one had ever heard him speak, or even make a noise, so it was generally assumed that he was dumb. He attended the clinic at the Littlemore Psychiatric Hospital once a week, and it was said that he had attended Lady De Pomeroy's Care Home in Wallingford, both as a patient and, latterly, as a gardener. Although he had an English name, many of us suspected that he had not been born in this country, for long words seemed to baffle him. He did not live with the single Italian men at the big house, but rather lived like a hermit in a converted barn at the edge of the estate. He did not mingle or associate with anyone, but he was a good worker for all of that.

At about the same time that I was attending my National Service medical, Harry was clearing a flooded ditch by the main road when he heard a female voice calling out in a strange tongue. He looked around, but not seeing anyone, went back to work. However, he could not shake off the memory of the voice or the worry that something awful had happened.

He put down his spade and walked down the road to have a look — and then he saw it; a body lying motionless in the long grass of the verge, face down.

A wheelchair was wedged on its side in the flooded culvert and an old lady, with water already up to her shoulders, was desperately struggling to free herself from the wheelchair, which was locked as it was in the concrete "V" sides of the culvert.

Without hesitation, Harry leaped into the icy water. The torrent was so fierce that the shock of it took his breath away. Rotten twigs and drowned rats piled up against his chest, driven by the force of the rapidly rising water.

18

Summoning all his strength, Harry fought to dislodge the wheelchair, but his attempts were hindered by the bags festooning the chair, which, as they swelled with water, served to further lodge her in.

After what must have been a superhuman effort, he managed to drag the old lady, still in her wheelchair, to the safety of the tarmac road.

It was at that moment that help arrived in the form of the Misses Franklin and their pony cart.

They quickly assessed the situation, and, with a decisiveness that made them the admiration of every single man in the village, they sprang out and immediately applied artificial resuscitation to the old lady, who by now was fading in and out of consciousness. The ladies lifted her into the pony trap and made her as comfortable as possible.

The older Miss Franklin, Annette, now turned her attention to the body in the grass — the lady's son. Against all odds, she discovered a weak pulse. It transpired that he had passed out from sheer exhaustion, probably aggravated by lack of food and his efforts to get his mother out of the driving rain.

Dr George Balassa had been driving up from Wallingford Hospital when he approached the scene and was waved down by Annette. His partner, Dr Julia Keane, was with him, and she transferred into the pony cart to assist Miss Franklin, whilst Doctor Balassa stayed to render assistance to the son.

Harry helped lift the unconscious man into the car, and the doctor sped him to the Radcliffe Hospital, where he was placed in Intensive Care.

The old lady was installed in one of the main bedrooms in the Franklin house, where she hovered between life and death for over a week, during which time the two Franklin sisters intensively nursed her, taking it in turns to sleep in a camp bed by her side. Time after time, the old lady would call out in a strange language which was unintelligible to the sisters. This left them most distressed inasmuch as they could not tell what she was saying or what she wanted. There was one word that she called out so many times, the sisters came to recognise it — "Gethsemene!" But they had no idea what it meant.

On the second night, the whole house was woken by a furious barking. When one of the household's men went down to the front door to investigate, he was confronted by a large, unkempt and fierce-looking dog. The creature bounded past him, running straight up the stairs, where it clawed frantically at the sickroom door.

Susan Franklin, fearing that the door might be irrevocably damaged, lifted the latch, and the great dog burst in, leaping on her patient's bed and licking the old lady's face and hands in great distress. Then came a miracle; the old lady opened her eyes and tried to sit up.

The dog settled down protectively at the foot of the patient's bed, who was now looking about her in wonder at the magnificent room. She was tearful with joy at being reunited with her dog.

C.J. had started the day in a particularly foul mood, having discovered that his flower garden had been destroyed during the night. Apparently, it looked as though a herd of cows had trampled the beds, but he was at a loss as to whose; Not his, surely, he reasoned, for they were in a field half a mile away. The hedges were good, and the gate was new, and, although it was not padlocked, it had a good latch.

As he looked on, a young bull hove into view with half a line of ruined washing caught round his horns. One of his young bulls! It was almost certain that someone had opened the gate during the night and driven the whole herd down the road and into his garden.

Daylight examination showed only the prints of a large dog among the cattle, but no human footprints.

C.J. rang Wallingford Police Station and was told that he would be prosecuted for leaving cattle on the road unattended (apparently Saunder's milk float had collided with one of the other steers. The animal was unhurt, but the float was extensively damaged). This made him furious. Remembering that the dog was taken to the pound, a shaken C.J. demanded, "Is that dog still there? Has it been destroyed as it should have been?"

"The dog is no longer with us," was the tart reply. This was no officer that C.J. could bribe, although to give him his due, he did try. Six months later, he received a six-month prison sentence, together with (according to my mother when she related the events to me when I came home on leave) some very unwelcome publicity about his dealings.

Apparently, the dog had settled calmly into the little shed where the police constables kept their bicycles. The door had a latch some four feet off the ground. The dog ate a hearty, well-deserved meal, and then settled down for the night. But during the night, the latch had been softly lifted, and the bird had flown. Strangely, the door had been softly closed again. The loss was not discovered until 8a.m. the next morning, and by then, they were too busy to worry about a runaway dog, which no one (apart from C.J.) considered to be even remotely dangerous.

Henry Smith

But what about Henry? He had risked his life rescuing an old lady from certain death. The old lady was being cared for at the big house (there were actually two big houses — one at each farm, but only the one where the Franklin sisters lived was known as *the* big house).

Still soaking wet and shivering from the cold, he had collected the bags of possessions from the culvert and placed them in a soaking pile on the other side of the farm hedge, carefully concealing them from curious passersby. He then took up the bicycle, swung his ditching tools in a sack around his shoulders and made wet and unsteady progress to the big house.

Much to the delight of several giggling housemaids, he was promptly ordered by the formidable housekeeper into a large zinc bath placed in front of the kitchen log fire. The lady had lost a son in the Italian Resistance, and she saw a strong resemblance in Henry and had kept a motherly eye on him ever since he had arrived at the farm some months earlier.

One of the girls was sent to his cottage to fetch a fresh change of clothes, and yet another volunteered to launder the clothes he had been wearing.

Later on, washed, dressed and warm, he was in the great kitchen, where the enormous table was laden with beautiful china and delicious dishes of food. He was feted in style by every one of the farm staff who had come to shake the hand of their hero, and Dr Julia Keane had popped in to give him a quick checkover and pronounced that "no ill effects were suffered".

About half past two, the local district nurse called in to see the new patient. Annette was telling her the story, when the nurse suddenly said, "You did not say anything about the handcart. I am sure that someone told me that they also had a handcart."

The two sisters had not been aware of the missing item, and so two farm labourers were despatched to find it. It was duly discovered pushed into a lane in Nuneham Courtenay, where it had been concealed in a wooded entrance. One of its wheels had partially jammed on its axle, and, stacked as it was with old suitcases, boxes and a brass bedstead and a horsehair mattress, the two of them could barely shift it.

Now, a few weeks earlier, the sisters had taken delivery of not one, but four new tractors — the latest thing in modern farming, and the Italian labourers, with whom the tractors had proven to be a big hit, needed no urging to bring one of the machines up to tow the cart slowly and carefully into the farm coach yard.

The six magnificent shire horses had been put into well deserved semi retirement on the farm, where they were growing fat and lazy.

The tractors had proved to be a great hit with the Italian labourers, any one of whom needed no excuse to service or drive these wonderful machines, as Mr Wyatt the farm manager remarked. It seems that every Italian male has motor oil running through his veins; they were so keen to show what these machines could do that productivity went up by 200 per cent.

Many a late night, Italian housewives came out to drag their husbands into cold dinners on tables laid several hours earlier and with children sound asleep in their beds.

The situation got so involved, that in the end the dozen aspiring mechanic drivers were put to a test, the winners would each have a tractor under their charge.

It needed no urging to bring a tractor up to tow the cart slowly and carefully into the farm coach yard, and it was when it was being unhitched, that one of the axles, notably the one belonging to the wheel that was jamming, gave up the struggle and collapsed completely.

Apart from the horsehair mattress, everything was dry, having been tied down under the tarpaulin. The whole load was packed by willing hands into a particularly dry corner of the large Georgian coach house which was empty apart from Bertolli's workshop and a beautiful gypsy caravan which was being slowly and meticulously restored by that craftsman.

Bertolli, or "Bert" as everybody called him, was a sixty-year-old Italian craftsman, who had, he boasted, worked on Milan Cathedral. He had come to England to stay with his son, Mario, and his family, who had come to the farm as a prisoner of war, and was now, some ten years later, the senior foreman of both farms.

Bert had lost his wife to cancer some five years earlier and was now, it was rumoured, romantically involved with a widow in Littlemore Parish.

He acted as maintenance man to the two farms, and the sisters had extensively equipped the coach house with an array of the latest woodworking machines, as well as a small forge and blacksmith's shop. This was Bert's kingdom, and he was probably the happiest man in England; he had around him his family and his grandchildren, who all adored him. For years, he had lived in a poor and rather grimy district in Milan, and now he lived in the elegant coachman's cottage on the estate, with swans at his front door, wood pigeons in the woods behind him and a little cabin cruiser moored into the backwater at the end of his kitchen garden.

It was soon to be Annette's birthday, and the whole household wanted to give their beloved mistress a celebration to remember.

For many years, there had been a real Romany camp at Sandford upon Thames, just down the road. The gypsies, who for generations had acted as fruit and potato pickers on the farms, had sold Mario the aforementioned gypsy cart that Bert was now restoring and transforming into a wonderful work of art.

The Franklin sisters protested that they did not celebrate birthdays or Christmas, but "Little Tuscany" would have none of it.

"I'm rather afraid that it is a case of liking it or lumping it," Annette had said to Susan. They had tried, in vain, to explain to their extended family that their beliefs did not allow them to celebrate Christmas or birthdays, only wedding anniversaries.

This had, unfortunately, upset the children, who had been looking forward to meeting Father Christmas. In the end, the sisters had capitulated, and the children had had their way; although, of course, the sisters had not joined in the celebrations.

Annette was well aware of her proposed birthday present, and often went to watch Bert at his labour of love. In the end, the sisters hit upon a solution.

"British kings and queens have two birthdays — an official one and a private one. I shall put my birthday a week ahead, and that will be my official 'unbirthday'. Hopefully no one will suspect a thing," Annette had said.

Bert had extended both the body and the shafts of this wonderful vehicle. He had replaced the wooden wheels with the latest in motor-van wheels, a brake pedal and a handbrake placed by the driver's seat, plus a modern electrical system to make the caravan road legal. The interior was a model of design. Cunningly designed cupboards and wardrobe doors concealed all those implements needed for living on the road. The wives had painstakingly sewn beautiful curtains and cushions. The interior surfaces were elegantly veneered in Fiddleback Mahogany, and there was even a tiny kitchen galley with a wood burning stove and a working water tap.

It was because the weight had been nearly doubled, that the vehicle had had its shafts extended to take not one, but two, of the great shire horses.

Henry Smith spent a lot of time either training the horses to work in tandem or helping Bert with the painting and polishing. Bert had a fine tenor voice and fancied himself as an opera singer. Henry had a guitar, and he was not long under Bert's influence before his confidence began to blossom, and the pair started to give impromptu concerts on the lawn in front of Bert's cottage.

There was one incident when Henry and Bert had gone to the house of Bert's intended, and, creeping outside her window, had serenaded her by moonlight. Unfortunately for them, the lady, who had taken a sleeping pill, was quietly snoring in the back bedroom. Her old and somewhat cantankerous mother was asleep in the front bedroom, and hers was the window they had chosen to serenade under.

At least a dozen neighbours, attracted by the noise, had come out into their front gardens to watch. Bert, who had dressed himself in a borrowed "Pirates of Penzance" costume and had glued on a stiff waxed moustache for effect, sang for at least half an hour, whilst the neighbours cheered and clapped each aria.

Fuelled by a bottle of red wine, he sang until it looked as if the sash around his waist, tight as it was over his portly frame, would burst. But there was not even a twitch from the bedroom window.

"Give me a sign, my love!" he called, beseechingly.

And then the sash window flew up. Spreading his arms joyfully and raising his face towards the window, he cried, "She is here! My love! Will you . . . ?"

Before he could complete the sentence, he received a cascade of water in his upturned face.

"Let that be a lesson to you, you Italian varmint! Disturbing an old woman's sleep at this time in the morning; hop it before I call the police!"

A malicious gnome face appeared at the window, hair in curlers looking like a barbed-wire fence and a face covered in white face powder. It was a face you could frighten rats with.

"Be off you heathen, or you will get another one!"

They left hurriedly, whilst his lady friend slept on, blissfully unaware.

The Bully and the Bedsprings

I awoke early, having barely slept. Today was the day I joined the army. Not as a volunteer, but as a national serviceman. I could hear Mum downstairs getting the family breakfast and my father, who was a First World War veteran, scrubbing up his old army kitbag, in which I would carry my spare clothes, etc. Mother presented me with an almighty breakfast, convinced that I was going to starve on army fare. Dad presented me with my shoes, buffed to a high shine.

At 7.25, I pried myself from my mother's tearful embrace, and Dad and I set out for Littlemore Railway Station, Dad pushing his old bike, upon the handlebars of which was balanced the kitbag. Dad was as proud as a dog with two tails, raising his cap to all our neighbours, for this was the day that I, his son, came of all.

The railway station was roughly about half a mile from the house. My dad always swore that the British railway system was the finest asset this country had ever had. Every UK destination was now no more than a 20-minute walk and a train ride away. Anyway, there we were, striding out to the railway station, me carrying a brown carrier bag with enough sandwiches for a fortnight, and my father with his freshly scrubbed kitbag balanced upon his bike.

We had not gone two hundred yards when we saw a small figure dodge behind a large bush in a neighbour's garden.

"Jimmy Twp!" we both exclaimed. At that moment he took to his heels, an object clutched under his shapeless coat.

"At least that explains who has been stealing the milk," said my father. "Poor little devil!"

We all knew Jimmy Twp (pronounced "Tup"). Ever since I could remember, he had been a fixture around the streets of Rosehill.

"Carry your shopping for tuppence missus?" and he would bob and clutch his cap, twisting it in two grimy hands, eager to please. Less that 4′ 6″ in stature, he moved everywhere at a sort of high-speed hobble. Although Dad reckoned that he was in his thirties, he had a simple, child-like mentality. I don't know if he had a father; we never saw one. His mother, with whom he had lived, had been an elderly, diminutive little lady, habitually dressed in black, and who kept herself to herself. Her house had been neat as a pin, like herself — windows, hung with floral curtains, sparkled; tiny lawns, smooth as velvet; and a garden with such a profusion of vegetables and flowers, even father was envious. Six months ago, Mrs Twp had died, leaving Jimmy to fend for himself. Either forgotten or overlooked by the local authorities, he and the house in which he lived were slowly descending into wrack and ruin.

We headed on past the church and my two old primary schools, over the bridge and down the long slope to the railway station.

Littlemore Station was a jewel in the crown of the Great Western Railway. The painted surfaces around the building and its bright wicket fence sparkled. The two porters and the booking clerk, immaculate in their railway uniforms, were busy polishing the many brass handles, whilst the lady booking clerk was watering the baskets of flowers which hung in such profusion around the platform, which appeared to have been thoroughly scrubbed earlier. Such was the standard of cleanliness at the station, Father swore that the stationmaster's wife had been polishing the rails with silver polish, and there were those of his friends who believed him.

The stationmaster now appeared, resplendent in his uniform of gold-braided peaked cap and brass-buttoned jacket, stiff starched collar and shiny boots.

"Morning Frank," said he. "This the big day for the young master?"

I blushed furiously, as I thought, "Condescending old fool!"

My father saw what was in my mind, but as I said it, my furious retort was completely lost in the stentorian bellow of our railway engine as it emerged from under the bridge, much to my father's relief.

Our transport consisted of two streamlined diesel cars which were brightly painted in the Great Western livery. Both cars were identical and were what Doctor Dolittle might have referred to as a "pushmi-pull yu". All the driver had to do at the end of his journey was to walk down from his cab, drop into the rear facing driver's seat and he was ready to return home, without having to turn the train around.

Father quickly pushed my kitbag up onto the seats just behind the driver. The interior was similar to a bus.

The stationmaster boarded the carriage behind us.

"Good morning, Mr Belcher," he said to the driver, producing a large silver pocket watch. "This won't do!" he said sternly. "One minute and twenty-seven seconds late! This is the second time in two years. That time you were two minutes late! Absolutely disgusting. We shall be getting a reputation for unreliability if you don't pull your socks up my man."

Mr Belcher scowled. "Don't blame me, Mr Clifton; blame Thames Station! The idiots up there left the ladies lavatories locked; someone mislaid the key. I had to pull up in a cutting to let the ladies relieve themselves behind the low bushes."

"Right," said Mr Clifton, studying his watch. "You have exactly one minute and seventeen seconds for departure. You will leave directly upon my whistle!"

Meanwhile, the two porters were dashing along the length of the two carriages slamming their doors, finishing up with the door I was seated against. The stationmaster raised a small green flag and there was an impressive blast from his whistle. The driver responded with a toot from his engine's horn and two raised fingers at the stationmaster's retreating back, and we were off.

I waved from the open window to my father, who managed to keep pace with the train for nearly twenty-five yards on his old bike, going at such a pace I was afraid that he might ride off the end of the station platform. He did manage to stop however, and a second later, he was lost from sight.

We passed a gang of railway workers all standing back from the track and who, as we passed, saluted us with mugs of what I presumed was strong tea. A minute later, we were sliding across the river Thames, over the black bridge and powering down to Oxford.

Bicycles littered the gangways, trilby-hated gentle-men studied newspapers and chomped upon cigars, and several knots of ladies, dressed in their Sunday best, chattered excitedly, presumably looking forward to an exciting shopping expedition. There were two backpackers, all sun-bronzed knees, gleaming teeth, and earnest expressions as they studied guidebooks and maps. There were also half a dozen lads of about my age. In due course, I was to discover that they were, like myself, conscripts to the King's army.

We passed the mainline signal box. One signalman was hanging out of the high window cleaning it; a second one could be glimpsed at the signal levers, and a third one was sat upon the outside platform on the tall steps of the signal box, checking a list. Seconds later we had crossed the bridge, and we were at journey's end — Oxford station.

We all got off. There were quite a lot of people milling about on the platforms and there must have been at least sixty young men congregated just inside the booking room. All were of my age, and each carried either a suitcase or a backpack. In my case, I had a kitbag. It dawned on me that these were to be my new travelling companions.

A very impressively uniformed army Sergeant materialised in our midst. "Right gentlemen! I will call out your names, and as they are called out, you must answer, "Yes Sergeant," and then form a line at the north end of the platform."

The roll call was made in alphabetical order, and so I was last to join the line. We were then informed that we had twenty minutes before our train arrived, and, when it did, we were to take the first two carriages in the order we were called up in, and that we could fall out for a smoke. I did not smoke, so I popped into the buffet shop on the platform and got a very welcome cup of tea. The Sergeant also had the same idea, and he generously paid for the beverage. In the course of our conversation, I learned that we were to entrain to the Royal Artillery Induction Camp in Oswestry, Shropshire.

The train rushed through the countryside at sixty miles an hour. We sat in subdued blocks of six, our luggage stored under the seats, with small bags and boxes above in net hammocks. Every so often, a smoky blast of air would enter through the top sliding windows, so that we were slowly being covered in black smuts. After a couple of hours, I shared out my sandwiches to the seated compartment. It seemed that my mother knew what she was doing, because I seemed to be the only one to have brought food with me.

All too soon, we arrived at Oswestry, and there, again, we had to detrain and muster on the railway platform, complete with luggage. There must have been well over one hundred of us, and now we were required to get onto three coaches, obviously hired for the purpose. With the luggage loaded, we were again on our way.

My first impression of the Royal Artillery Camp was that of a dozen or so modern hangar-like buildings, each covering around an acre of concrete flooring, some open to the sides. There were lethal-looking dark-green field guns everywhere, with neat canvas hoods over their barrels and stacks and stacks of artillery shells. Squads of denim suited men marched everywhere, barked at by over-enthusiastic Sergeants and their assistant Bombardier, whilst their victims struggled to comply with their shouted commands and, occasionally, even managed to march in step.

The largest of the buildings was what they designated a dining or "mess" hall. It was similar to the other buildings, except that it had four permanent walls with a stage platform at one end and, at the other, a huge kitchen with cooks toiling away. In the middle area were long lines of trestle tables and chairs.

Again, a roll call was taken, and we then had to file past an elderly tea urn to collect a none-too-clean battered tin mug and a dollop of strong, brown and mysterious liquid.

"Is this tea or coffee?" we asked.

"It's whatever you want it to be!" came the smug reply of the soldier manning the tea urn. "One thing though — drink this, and you will forget all about women. The only oats you will get in this establishment is porridge, salty as the Irish Sea and great for polishing your brasses!"

There now came an announcement from the overhead loud speakers for us to take our places at the tables, upon which we would find neatly printed cards bearing our names. We were not to sit down, but were required to stand to some sort of attention whilst dozens of Sergeants passed behind us, each carrying trays of beer in half pint glasses. These were placed upon the tables in front of us, with the admonition that they were not to be touched before the order was given.

As we were standing at right angles to the stage, we could now see several impressive-looking Officers upon it, the chief of which now addressed us. I forget the actual words, except that it was a welcoming speech, stressing the traditions and benefits of being in the Royal Artillery. When he had finished, we were then addressed by the Padre or Army Chaplain, who, irrespective of individual beliefs, led us in a short prayer. The Adjutant now stepped forward, and he pronounced the oath of allegiance to God, King and Country, which we all repeated line by line and word for word. Finally we were ordered to drink a toast to the King and then to the Regiment. We stood facing the stage, and following the example of the Regimental Sergeant Major, we each raised our glasses in our right hands and took two hearty swigs. At the bottom of my glass, something could be seen glinting, and upon further investigation, it proved to be an old silver shilling piece — the King's Shilling! Now having drunk the King's beer, we were deemed to be new members of the Royal Regiment of Artillery.

A large stack of tin trays was now placed at the end of each table, and these were passed along one by one until each seated man had received one. I looked at mine curiously. About the size of a domestic tea tray, it had shallow compartments hammered into it, the reason for which soon became clear. We were then passed a battered enamel mug and a clip containing a knife, fork and spoon. I found myself lining up in front of the food server. Two men stood on the opposite side of the table behind a large steaming dish of carrots and another one of boiled potatoes. The scene was repeated at regular intervals along the table, with pairs of soldiers doling out dollops of carrots, peas, cabbage and turnips, together with a very watery looking stew. Beyond these were another two stations serving up bread and margarine, rice pudding, custard and apple crumble. The resulting mess in each tray looked revolting. So speedily was each item slopped into the tray, custard intermingled with potatoes, gravy crowned the apple crumble and stew covered everything else and dribbled over the shallow edges of the trays. To add to the general chaos, scores of sparrows and starlings flew around, or roosted in the high-girded ceiling and let their droppings fall with depressing frequency, much of which landed in the food. The tea was pretty awful as well; black as tar, it had been brewed up in a huge vat, to which condensed milk had been added together with the tins, which were simply split in half with a fireman's axe and dropped straight into the noxious brew. The tins were presumably collected when the vats were cleaned out.

We were given ten minutes to finish our meal and then were required to clean our dishes. By the exit doors was a large water tank, half full of hot water, into which half a sack of soda crystals had been dropped. Above it, dangling on cords, were half a dozen scrubbing brushes for cleaning our "eating irons". Woe betide anyone who dropped an item and had to grope around in the tank's soupy depths.

Once we'd washed up, we were allocated our sleeping quarters. These were wooden buildings called "spiders". They were huts joined at right angles to a central section which contained lavatories, wash and shower rooms and a scrubbing room for kit cleaning. Each room contained twenty beds, ten on each side of a central aisle. The beds were situated at regular intervals and were flanked on either side by a metal wardrobe and bedside locker. Once inside, we chose our beds, slid our bags underneath, and put our names on the cards affixed to each frame.

A Sergeant then summoned us back outside, and we lined up in our alphabetical order. Thus arranged, we marched to the Quartermaster's store, which was a huge building with a long counter spanning its length. Behind the counter were rank upon rank of lockers and shelves. These contained all sorts of army clothing: boots, belts, haversacks and other webbing. Manning the counter were about a dozen soldiers, a Sergeant and an Officer. We were instructed to file slowly down the length of the counter, stopping at each store man. I saw no sign of a tape measure — the store man simply measured us up with a practised eye. Step by step, we were issued with two pairs of everything: shirts, ties, underpants, cellular vests, socks, trousers, battle dress blouses and all sorts of essential equipment. Eventually, loaded up like donkeys, we staggered to the end of the counter and out of the door.

Once we'd arrived back at our respective barrack rooms, the bargaining began in earnest. There were a great many different body shapes on view — tall, short, fat, thin — and it was soon found that very few of my companions had been given uniforms that remotely fitted. I myself had received a battledress two sizes too short and trousers that flapped over my shoes. The swapping and bargaining continued until we were all reasonably attired in the uncomfortable khaki battledress (we soon discovered that whatever the material had been treated with brought many of us out in an ugly rash, myself included), by which time we were due to return to the mess hall (so very aptly named!) to eat an indigestible liver and bacon dish, liberally spattered with brown Windsor soup, followed by apple and rice pudding.

On our return, the Bombardier instructed us to write a letter home on the notepaper that he was now issuing. My neighbour was distressed, because, as he quietly explained to me, he had no writing skills. I told him to tell me what he wanted to say, and I wrote it for him.

For some time, I had been uncomfortably aware of a youth, slightly bigger than myself, who seemed to have taken a dislike to me. It transpired that he came from

Nottingham, and, according to him, he was a member of a particularly violent and sadistic gang. He seemed to go out of his way to barge into me "accidently". I recognised the situation for what it was. My father had warned me about the barrack-room bullies.

"The world," he used to say, "is divided into victims and predators; be neither."

I took care to avoid the youth, but the more I tried to ignore him, the worse he became. He sneeringly referred to me as the "Oxford Ponce". Anyway, I was not particularly perturbed by him; I had spent my early years as a grammar schoolboy defending myself against some of the roughest gangs in the Midlands, and, as a result, I had not only represented my school in the semi-finals of the Amateur Boxing Association at Eton College, I could also hold my own in the more brutal "no holds barred" street fighting culture of the day; so I did not feel unduly threatened.

A quarter of an hour before "lights out", having made my bed and stowed my things neatly in the locker, I went for a shower. When I returned, I realised that something very strange had happened. The excited chatter, which had so filled the room when I left, had been replaced with an expectant, deathly hush. Feeling all eyes upon me, I ventured deeper into the room, and realisation dawned; the old days were not consigned to the past — I would have to fight my corner, yet again.

There upon my bed lay the gangster. My clothes were strewn all about the floor, and my kitbag had been upended into a rather smelly wastebasket.

For a moment, I shook with white hot rage, and I took a step towards the offender. Then I recalled my father's voice.

"Calm right down. Think the situation through, and then humiliate him so much that you will destroy his credibility; never get mad, get even!"

Somehow, I kept my cool, nigh on impossible though it was, and I meekly gathered up my possessions into a pile in the middle of the room.

"This is my bed now, Ponce; you go down there."

There were some sniggers from our companions over my apparently wimpish behaviour. But how best to respond? Then it came to me. Whilst still an apprentice in house furnishing at C.P. Webbers, I had been required to assist the porters in delivering, and assembling, several hundred bedsteads, mattresses, wardrobes and lockers to New College, Oxford. This was a particularly arduous job, because hundreds of twisting, worn stone stairs had to be negotiated, and hefting both the metal divan and spring interior mattress had demanded a certain degree of strength.

Those beds, I'd suddenly realised, were of a similar make to these army beds. My decision made, I walked over to his bed, picked it up, and strode over to where he was lying with a silly, self-satisfied smirk upon his face. It was unfortunate for him that his eyes were closed, otherwise he'd have seen it coming, as I lined up the bed and simply dropped it. The divan legs dropped over neatly, and he was pinned

"You've forgotten your bed!" I said loudly, as I added my fourteen-stone weight to the snare. The pain must have been considerable, as he screamed, shouted and swore, utterly incapable of relieving the situation.

After about five minutes, I relented and lifted the bed off; too soon, it seemed for he still had some fight in him. He launched himself off the bed, and I met him with a straight left, followed by a right cross. He dropped like a sack of potatoes.

"Who's next?" I demanded loudly, looking about, but there were no takers.

I picked up his equipment and threw it out through the nearest window, then I herded him back to his corner, where he sat, defeated, in the dark.

The following afternoon, we discovered that he had deserted, and I never saw him again.

Redcap

The next morning, after a breakfast of porridge and bird droppings, we were given our first taste of marching drill or "square bashing" as it was called. Drill took place in one of the cavernous hangers, from which the field guns had been hauled out in order to give us the space to develop our marching skills. A brigade of guards we were not. Most of the first session was spent trying to distinguish the left foot from the right. Inevitably, when trying to execute a "Right Turn" or even an "About Turn!", some confused individual would turn the wrong way and the rest of the squad would collapse into them. Our drill parades proved to be a great source of entertainment to the various cooks, A.T.S. typists and off-duty drill instructors, many of whom cried tears of laughter upon viewing our shambolic endeavours.

The rest of that day consisted of interviews, written examinations, lectures, a forty-minute run and then more marching. Lance Bombardiers visited the various dormitories that evening, in order to instruct us on such things as how to clean our kits, spit-polish boots until they gleamed like black jewels, polish brasses and the correct way on how to lay the uniform trousers beneath a mattress to gain the immaculate creases so beloved of the army.

* * *

The camp was surrounded by huge potato fields, and we were required to volunteer our services, collecting stones from the fields and gathering the crops themselves, such as potatoes, carrots, cabbages, depending on what was in season.

We were also required to learn our eight digit number, unique to each man, to such effect, that sixty years on, I can still bring it immediately to mind.

During that first week, like all my fellow recruits, I was interviewed by a bored lieutenant in order to ascertain what my particular duty should be in the King's Army.

The following Monday, I had my answer; I was to be sent to Rhyl to train as a Technical Assistant (field guns) — apparently a plum post, but I was horrified. It had been assumed that, because I had been a scholarship boy, I was good with figures. Not so! I am dyslexic, not with letters, but with numbers, to such an extent that mathematics was quietly dropped from my itinerary, and I took extra French instead. I had such faith in my incompetence that I visualised all sorts of awful tragedies, such as shelling the wrong positions, or getting the shell charges wrong.

I was quietly desperate when I confided my fears to the Bombardier in charge of our hut. He in turn spoke to the Drill Sergeant, who in turn spoke to the Regimental Sergeant Major. The Sergeant Major, or R.S.M. as he was called, interviewed me at length and, after giving me a simple (to him) geometry test, passed me on to the Adjutant. As I waited outside the Adjutant's office, I studied a poster on the wall. This was of an immaculately turned out Military Policeman on a motor cycle. There were also smaller inset figures of M.Ps on horseback, with dogs, jumping from aeroplanes, aboard boats and driving jeeps.

I had been told that the corps of Royal Military Police (or C.R.M.P.) never recruited directly, but only from regiments of the British Army and Royal Marines. I had always wanted to drive a motorcycle or a jeep and I saw this as my opportunity to learn for free. Accordingly, I spoke to the Adjutant and, after conferring with the R.S.M., he said he would give me a decision in good time.

Anxiously, I waited for his decision, but nothing happened. Day after day passed and still nothing. Two weeks later, our transfer papers came through, and I was still expected to go to Rhyl. Despondently, I boarded the coach with a group of fellow soldiers, resigned to my fate.

The coach started up and we were off! I don't suppose we had travelled more than a mile from the camp gates when a Military Police jeep swung into the path of the coach, forcing us to a sudden stop. A red-capped Sergeant appeared at the front of the gangway.

"Private Wicks," he shouted. "Come forward!"

It appeared that I had got my transfer after all, though by the looks I was getting from my travelling companions, I fear they may have suspected that I was some master criminal, arrested in the nick of time.

Soon I was transported to the Oswestry railway station with my kitbag, handed a set of papers and a rail ticket and sent on my way to Inkerman Barracks, Woking.

Legend had it that Inkerman Barracks was an old lunatic asylum, built for the criminally insane. The sign that hung over the guardhouse aptly illustrated this high-walled, grey-stone building, which was set all around a vast echoing square. Worn with age and barely discernible, it read, "Abandon Hope All You Who Enter Here". Some wag had written beneath, "Never Forget Where You Left Your Trousers!"

I was required to sit in the high-ceilinged waiting area of the Orderly Room office, alone at first, but soon joined by other soldiers, all from various regiments. There were Royal Marines and guardsmen, gunner, infantrymen and even a horse guardsman. There were 120 men in all. A few were national service recruits like myself, others were seasoned soldiers with campaign medals, and a few wore stripes, denoting non-commissioned officers. However, because we were now of one rank only, probationer M.P.s, the badged N.C.O.s had to remove their insignia. Some were old soldiers who had left the army, hadn't liked what they'd found, so had joined up again.

The first thing that struck me about the place was the noise. The curious high pitched yelps that echoed across the parade square made it remarkably reminiscent of a dog kennel; then I realised it was coming from some half a dozen drill instructors who were parading sweating groups of soldiers up and down the grey-cobbled surface.

We were divided into three separate squads of approximately forty men apiece. Each squad was under the control of a Sergeant and two physical training instructors or P.T.I.s as they were known. The P.T.I.s were sadistic brutes, who tormented us through unarmed combat and physical training. Within several days, we realised that they were power mad. One of their favourite ploys was to order each victim to have a haircut. I had had my hair cut short by an Oxford barber before joining up, but now I had to have four close-cropped haircuts within the space of three days, and I was not the only one. Every day there were long lines outside the camp hairdressers, to whom we had to hand a scrawled chit and one shilling and nine pence for a short back and sides. Several men, including myself, rebelled and were put on a charge for failing to comply with a direct military order. We were paraded in front of the Adjutant. We were not allowed to speak in our defence and were all given two hours late drill, including a full kit inspection, plus Sunday afternoon camp duties. Our particular camp duty, I recall, was to scrub about 9 square yards of gymnasium floor with a toothbrush — a common punishment. It turned out we were softly treated compared to those who had to scrub the toilet cubicles using their own toothbrushes.

Unarmed combat was the worst. We would be segregated into pairs, one soldier as the aggressor, the other as defender. If the P.T.I. felt that not enough pain was being inflicted upon the person receiving the hold, he would apply extra pressure. As a result of this, one man's wrist was broken, and he was sent away for 4 weeks leave.

The P.T.I.s also took great delight in pushing us into muddy trenches filled with water which we were traversing on the end of a rope.

The biggest brute of the lot was our drill instructor, a Northern Ireland Protestant from Belfast — Sergeant McShane (not his real name, I hasten to add). The grapevine told us that he had once been married, but his wife had divorced him after only three weeks. He was a man with a chest full of campaign medals and a mouth so foul, it was like listening to the screams of the damned trapped in hell. Unfortunately, one of the officer's wives objected to his strident epithets which carried over the parade ground in full hearing of the children's school run, and he was duly dressed down by her in front of us. After she had gone, he turned to us and said,

"Well, you heard the lady — does anyone else object to the King's English?"

I was not used to foul language; I worked in an environment where people did not swear. Rough as the district was, our neighbours did not swear, and my father and mother most certainly did not swear.

"Anyone objections to my language?" he asked again, in his sneering Belfast accent.

There was silence from the ranks, and then my brain switched off, and my mouth took over.

"Yes Sergeant, I do."

"What was that probationer?" he demanded.

I recalled my father's words that people who swear do not have the brains to express themselves properly; only cretins fill in the blanks with swear words as it makes them feel clever. In reality, they are uneducated slobs.

I relayed this information to him, while the rest of the squad sniggered. Two minutes later, I found myself on a charge marching between two escorts to the Adjutant's office, the Sergeant leading the way.

As we came to stand outside the Adjutant's office, we heard the shrill tones of the lady who had complained to sergeant McShane; obviously she was not happy with his response.

Sergeant McShane flushed an angry red, and, as the office clerks came outside to hear what all the commotion was about, we all grinned. Eventually, the door opened, and the lady emerged. Giving Sergeant McShane an icy stare, she stalked off, leaving him visibly shaken. Turning to myself and the escorts he shouted, "Caps off, belts off," and I was escorted into the Adjutant's office. We had to march into the office in double quick time, and our rapidly thudding army boots were so loud, they threatened to dislodge the ceiling plasterwork. The Adjutant, who was well known for liking a couple of snorts of whisky at lunchtime, put his head in his hands and directed at Sergeant McShane a look of pure malevolence as he listened, stony-faced to the Sergeant's charge of insubordination. I was not allowed to speak in my defence, and my punishment was to be confined to camp for one month, plus four weekends of kitchen fatigues.

I had come off lightly, although I did not appreciate it at the time. The Sergeant was ordered to stay behind, and it seemed that he also received a severe dressing down, because for a few days after, his language was severely curtailed. I, however, had made an enemy, and one who I could not fight. In his twisted mind, I was the reason for his downfall, and I became a target to his circle of cronies. Every day I was singled out for harsh criticism: My bed was half an inch over the white painted line; there was dust on the light fitting which hung a good ten feet above my bed; the shape of a button sewn on the reverse of the lapel had been pressed into visibility on the front side; crushed fibres had been imprinted by the smoothing iron — I got extra night fatigues for that one.

It was inevitable that I should stand out from the others because of my treatment, and those who wished to curry favour with their instructors took full advantage of it. I was having a pretty bad time of it.

There were in our group, six recruits from Liverpool, all of whom had been police cadets with the Liverpool Constabulary, and I began to hate them. If a cruel trick was played upon anyone, they were inevitably at the bottom of it. On one occasion, one of the gang had to clean out the general office, and he took it upon himself to snoop into the probationers' confidential records. He discovered that I had boxed in the interschool's boxing championships and that another probationer had also done the same in Yorkshire. It was therefore planned to pit us against each other to afford some illegal barrack entertainment for the rest, but I was sick of fighting,

51

and Frank felt the same, and so we became good friends. This did not suit the Liverpool "mafia" at all, who branded us cowards.

Finally, we hatched a plan. We would fight (but we carefully avoided saying "each other"). The set-to was scheduled for Easter Bank Holiday in the gymnasium. There was one condition — the match was to be refereed by the person who had accessed our records. This, he was delighted to do.

The day dawned, and we hammed it up like the great enemies we were supposed to be, but of course never were. "Scouser", the ref., grinned broadly as he bowed to his audience and informed us that he wanted a good clean fight. The bell was rung and we advanced upon each other. Scouser hopped around us like a demented rabbit, and, on cue, we hit him simultaneously. He dropped like a rock.

"Anyone else want to get involved?" Frank queried. Five minutes later the Liverpool "mafia" were fighting each other and everyone else, going at it with such ferocity, the ring threatened to collapse under the weight of bodies. Frank and I stood back and admired our handiwork.

"Fancy a char and a wad?" asked Frank. "My treat." And we strolled arm in arm to the N.A.A.F.I. for a cup of tea and a slice of cake.

If I had it bad, there were many others who were considerably worse off. One such lad was from Dublin, Ireland. It transpired that his father was English, and although he had never been to England before, he found himself in our squad in Inkerman Barracks. His father had been a guardsman, and without actually seeing him, the army decided that he should become a member of the Irish Guards. Unfortunately, no one had taken his dark skin tone into account (his mother was a second generation West Indian, and it was because of the prejudice shown to his wife, that the father had moved his small family to Dublin). Fearing the repercussions of a black face seen guarding Buckingham Palace, the army hierarchy had rapidly transferred "Paddy" into the camp.

Sergeant McShane led the witch hunt against him.

"Why don't you desert," was his constant taunt.

The Liverpool mafia, taking their cue from Sergeant McShane, used every cruel trick in the book to make his life miserable. His bed was carried out and left in the middle of the parade ground; his kit would frequently be vandalised; the P.T.I.s took great delight in putting him down, often addressing him as "Nigger Pat".

One day, he snapped and laid one of the P.T.I.s out cold. No one spoke up for him, and he was escorted to the guardroom. That night, four instructors entered the guardroom and beat him so severely that his spleen was ruptured. There was an immediate whitewash, and a statement was issued to the effect that he had suffered peritonitis, and we never saw him again.

As a result of this incident, however, the culprits were all swiftly packed off, and we received a new Sergeant, Sergeant Bennet, who was a far more humane figure; stern but fair and always approachable.

He was a medium sized, thickset man, with a cheerful expression and always, even on parade, accompanied by a small Springer Spaniel, whom he had trained to walk impeccably by his side. Legend had it that the dog had saved his life by sniffing out a booby trap. Under his tuition, our group prospered, and I began to enjoy the army.

I did not enjoy the cooking, though. We had plates and mugs, but only a sadist could have produced the meals which were dolloped out. The Corporal in charge of the canteen was an old soldier, who had been a prisoner of war in Japan during the last conflict, and he was still showing some bizarre behaviour. Every now and then, something would trigger him, and he would throw pots, plates and anything else that came to hand. He would often drop kick loaves of bread across the kitchen, aiming them to land in large wicker baskets behind the servers. Most of them missed, landing on the wet tiled floor. Unfortunately, these would then be served up with our meals. A young Second Lieutenant, who was called the Officer of the Day, and the Orderly Sergeant would sometimes make an appearance during the meal.

"Any complaints?" he shouted.

"No sir!" we shouted in unison, unable to take our eyes off a large moth caterpillar, all of three inches long, inching his stately way across Scouser's plate, intent upon a lettuce leaf. Scouser, meanwhile, was so intent upon talking and cramming food into his mouth that I do not believe that he was even aware of the caterpillar. A little while later, after some kindly soul had pointed out his misfortune, he headed at a rate of knots to the medical room, where he was put on a stomach pump. As Frank said afterwards, "it couldn't have happened to a nicer guy."

Our squads of 40 men each had been divided into three sections: the first section would receive motorcycle training; the second one would receive vehicle training; and those who already possessed current driving licences would undertake advanced heavy vehicle training, or P.S.V.

During this period, we all had to do a forced march from Woking to Salamanca Barracks in Aldershot, a matter of some fourteen miles. It was a matter of honour between each instructor as to who would get there first. Unlike the other Sergeants, who travelled up by jeep, Sergeant Bennet led by example. He strode out in front of his men, his faithful companion at his side. Half way along, we made an illegal stop at a pub, where he treated us all to a cold Shandy. We were worried. "You can't afford this Serge — you being a family man an' all. All these drinks must cost a fortune."

"Don't worry," he replied. "I've got fifty quid riding on this race. I know the other instructors — they won't have the sense to stop and will run their men into the ground. We shall have two more stops, and then we will leave them standing." And we did. We passed one group with two miles to go. The other group were in sight of the winning post when we ran past them. They had no response, and we were as fresh as daisies. Our Sergeant bought us all another one that night.

Sergeant Bennet had been posted in from Cairo, Egypt. Before the war he had been a young police constable before joining the wartime Military Police. In Cairo, he had been a Company Sergeant Major, but had taken a voluntary reduction in rank in order to return to the U.K. where his wife was receiving critical cancer care. Sergeant Bennet was a gentleman — he did not curse us, or put us under stress. He led rather than drove us, and as a result we became the top squad in the depot. I especially benefited, to such an extent that on a Sunday church parade, I was approached by the great R.S.M. Britain himself and informed that I had been recommended for an officer's course.

After the fourteenth week of training, we were required to yomp on a forced march with full equipment to Aldershot, some fourteen miles away, to take part in vehicle training.

"Yomping", by the way, is a mixture of fast marching and running — incredibly tiring. It was with great relief that we turned into the old cavalry barracks that was to be our base for the next month. There were three courses open to us, one of which was driving, usually a Bedford 15 cwt lorry, or a motorcycle. Our squad was to learn how to ride a motorcycle.

The barracks, or horse lines as they were called, consisted of some dozen Victorian buildings and were basically stables with barrack room accommodation above in the long two storey buildings. Although the horses were long gone, the barracks absolutely reeked of horse manure. Our sleeping accommodation consisted of one bare room, in which were four lines of basic metal beds with a green metal locker for each one. There were no curtains, so one dressed behind the open door of one's cabinet. The floor was of rough scrubbed pine. There was no heating, which was just as well considering the smell of horses, mingled with the overpowering reek of petrol and oil fumes.

Our barracks would have been a modern Health and Safety Officer's nightmare. At each end of the room was a single door, behind which was an external iron staircase, which was lethal when it rained because of the smooth iron steps. Eventually, one staircase was roped off and used, instead, to store petrol containers.

Below in the old stables, sixty odd motorcycles were jammed into the confined spaces. Cigarette butts littered the floors. It was a miracle that there was never a serious fire as everybody seemed to smoke, and I even saw a mechanic working on a motorcycle with a lit cigarette dangling from his mouth, completely oblivious to the fact that there was an open petrol tank within just a few feet of him.

For the next month, we were to receive 4 hours per day motorcycle training. Sergeant Bennet still took drill training and police lecture, but every morning we would spend hours learning to ride the heavy B.S.A. girder forked motorcycles. These were slow, ponderous brutes with side-valved 500 c.c. engines that sounded like tractors and a sump clearance so low, that when doing cross-country training over rough terrain, they would suddenly stop on severed tree branches hidden in the long grass. It was a common sight to see a motorcycle travelling at thirty miles an hour stop abruptly, pitching its unfortunate rider into a graceful swallow dive into the rough grass beyond. We learned how to dismantle and replace a carburettor in seconds with a machine gun firing a few inches over our heads. We rode on handle bars, or dropped behind our moving motorcycles, whilst endeavouring to hit a moving target towed behind Sergeant Bennet's jeep with the most inaccurate pistol in the British Army. As our Colonel said, "They may not frighten the criminals, but by George, they terrify me!"

Attached to our squad was a Royal Signals Corporal named Corporal Moon, who was a large, beefy individual. He was aptly named as he had a big round face and a stomach which preceded him, or sat comfortably over his petrol tank. He was not well liked, as he had a cruel sense of humour. He was responsible for our motorcycle training, but he was an idiot. Nobody laughed but him. One day, the parade ground was set around with obstacles — beer barrels and the like. Each man was required to negotiate these obstacles, while riding at a walking pace, twisting around and between them whilst avoiding each one by less than three feet. We had to ride round and around the obstacles until he was satisfied that we could control our bikes before going out on the open road.

We all wore dispatch rider helmets, made of heavy steel, without visors. The trouble was that my helmet, in accordance with the army custom, was at least three sizes too big for me and there was no opportunity to change it. We wobbled around the course until Moon decided to relieve the boredom by producing a police-issue truncheon and hitting each rider on the helmet as they passed him. The result was that instead of maintaining concentration, several ran into the obstacles, with at least one person falling off.

Galvanised by this success, he grew even more enthusiastic, and as I passed him, he hit me hard on the helmet with all the force of his muscular arm. To me, it was like being in a dustbin whilst being hit with a sledgehammer. The interior of the helmet's webbing gave way and the helmet jammed down firmly over my eyes and nose. I lost control, but before I did, I managed to steer the motorcycle front mudguard into his bowed legs. Yes, I was hurt, with a broken wrist and a searing headache, but his injuries outweighed mine. Moon's riding jodhpurs were ripped to shreds, and he was cut in a particularly sensitive area. As I lay in the medical centre waiting for my wrist to be set, I had the satisfaction of listening to his shrieks as his wounds were treated none too gently with iodine.

My accident meant that my motorcycle training was finished. It was decided that I would assist Sergeant Bennet as much as possible, the result being that I came top of the written examinations. After two weeks, having lost so much in motorcycle training, the decision was taken to put me on a Bedford 15 cwt lorry in order to obtain a driving licence. All Military Policemen had to be proficient in the use of either the two wheeled or four wheeled vehicles. Sergeant Bennet had had the use of a Bren Gun Carrier and a jeep during his short stay in Cairo.

Whilst living in Cairo, Egypt, he had jumped upon his motorcycle, which was parked outside his married quarters, only to discover that a young cobra had crawled along the top of the bike's exhaust system for warmth during the night.

"I had a plastic windscreen on that bike, and I must have vaulted clear over the top of it," he told us.

I passed my driving test, scraping through the test for four-wheeled vehicles in a little military pick-up truck.

All too soon, the summer had passed, and it was time for our passing out parade. We spent all our free time polishing our brasses with near industrial levels of Brasso. We cleaned our brass buttons using a small nailbrush and a brass slide under the button to protect the uniform fabric. We rubbed our cap badges on pieces of cardboard liberally splashed with Brasso, until they were abraded so much that the fine details on the badges were flattened, producing a highly lustrous surface.

The camp tailors visited us, and we were issued with a new uniform, each one tailored to fit. Each jacket sported the single stripe or chevron denoting our new rank and the plum red badge of the C.R.M.P. Old soldiers showed us how to treat the inside of trouser creases with hand soap, which would produce a sharp, permanent knife-like crease. Our pistol holsters, belts, haversacks and gaiters were blanched white so many times, we were in danger of snow blindness.

Every night, we would sit around in groups, polishing our boots to a mirror shine. We achieved this by first smoothing out the leather using a hot silver spoon, which had been heated over a candle, and half a tin of Cherry Boot Polish. The resultant shine was produced by applying thin multiple layers of spit and a tiny quantity of polish applied with the forefinger and a soft duster. Chin straps and gaiter straps also received the same treatment. All our packs were neatly squared off with pieces of cardboard for fillings. Our pistols were so liberally oiled and polished that if we were to draw them in an emergency, they would most likely have slipped out of our grasp.

The anti-snake gaiters were the worst — they had a tendency to ride up over the tops of the boots with normal use, causing painful welts on the backs of our legs. We countered this by hanging lead weights inside the folds of the trouser bottoms, which helped to keep the gaiters in place, but having lead weights around your ankles is not the cleverest thing to do, as many ex-national servicemen still bear the scars of this dangerous practice. True, they made the trousers hang correctly, but that's about all. Probably the worst thing was the use of strips of leather in place of the usual bootlaces; they had the tensile strength of wool and were always breaking during drill, but substituting normal bootlaces in place of these standard army issue thin strips of leather could earn you a night's fatigues.

On inspection days, our mattresses were squared off with boards to give a flat, boxed-off appearance, likewise our two blankets and one pillow. Our kit also had to be displayed on the bed for minute inspection. It was common practice to set the whole thing up before going to bed at night, then sleeping on the bare boards underneath our beds to avoid disturbing the displays.

Our barrack room had a large grate, and this had to be scrubbed clean even into the chimney flue. There was a highly polished brass coal scuttle and each piece of coal set therein had to be carefully washed, dried and set back in place. Floors and walls had to be scrubbed till our arms ached. Piles of coke for the canteen had to be set in geometrically precise pyramids within painted white lines to denote their boundaries.

Windows were washed so many times that it was commonplace for birds to fly into them. We balanced precariously upon one another's shoulders to clean light fittings and cross beams. We hid the old brooms and scrubbing brushes and replaced them with new ones protected in cellophane. Heaven help anyone if a Sergeant Major came in, and wiping one finger upon a hidden ledge, came up with a single speck of grime upon one white gloved finger. No wonder men collapsed from exhaustion on the parade grounds on the following days' passing out parade.

Passing Out Parade

We woke to a beautiful September morning. This was the day that we would officially become Military Policemen. Practically all of us were awake and about well before the reveille buglers' call. We jostled each other to shave in the too few washbasins before the hot water ran out. Military washbasins were not equipped with drain plugs to the basins, and some old soldiers had learned to keep rubber bungs in a trouser pocket. The usual practice was to let what little hot water there was run free and unused straight down the wastepipes. We scraped at stubbly beards with single edged heavy-duty galvanised razor blades and used the army issue all-purpose hand soap in lieu of shaving foam. This soap was also used for scrubbing our kit and washing what little hair we had. The soap itself was a curious khaki colour and proved more hazardous than beneficial, as quite a few developed skin complaints after using it.

Sergeant Bennet came in to give a last minute pep talk.

"Chins in — chests out!" he said, and, "Bags of swank boys — bags of swank!"

Finally, after inspecting one another with a critical eye, we trooped out, bandy legged (to avoid damaging our boots and white gaiters by contact with each other) and stiff as marionettes (to keep our neatly pressed uniforms in pristine condition, and also because of the military white belts, worn so tight that they were as unyielding as a corset) onto the parade ground.

We duly paraded under the eagle eye of Sergeant Bennet, and then at 10.00a.m. precisely, in marched the lone piper of the Scots Guards. The order to march was given, the echoes rebounded back, and we marched once round the full parade ground and then out through the archway of the main gate and guardroom, where the full military band of the Scots Guards awaited to precede us.

Down the road we marched. "Bags of swank boys!" Sergeant Bennet had said, and bags of swank we gave it. We looked good, and we felt even better.

The children of the school came out to wave little Union Jack flags at our passing, and young mothers with pushchairs tried to keep up with our marching. The lone piper slipped away behind the trunk of a big chestnut tree for a crafty drag on a cigarette, and the band played on.

We wheeled smartly onto the big sports ground at the side of the barracks. In the middle of the field was a platform, upon which were set two dozen odd chairs and, in front of that, a "saluting" lectern. Around this were masses of flowers in pots and troughs and, all hung side by side, the flags of the Union Jack, the C.R.M.P. and the General Officer Commanding Aldershot District. Around the roped-off boundary were hundreds of chairs occupied by hundreds of spectators. Behind these lines were pavilions, first aid posts, beer tents, and latrines, to name but a few.

The Provost Marshal himself was to take the salute, and we marched past, half strangling ourselves to give an "eyes right" and at the same time not stumble upon the soft grass. Eventually, we were up in ranks in front of the Colonel and one by one we had to march smartly towards him. Saluting stiffly, but smartly, we had to shout out our serial number, rank name and initials, before being presented with the official M.P. armband and Redtop. Having put these on and saluted smartly yet again, we strode back to the ranks.

How I wished that my father could have seen my moment of triumph. There were masses of my colleagues' relatives and girlfriends present, many of whom had arrived by private car or taxi, but I knew that there was no way that my family could hope to afford the coach or train fare. I was so disappointed, and then felt ashamed of myself. I didn't know how far Woking was from Oxford, but I did know that it was an awfully long way.

We were marched back to our barrack room to take off our white accoutrements and to return our pistols to the armoury, and then it was off to the canteen for a surprisingly half-decent meal. Afterwards, we were free to do whatever we liked.

I couldn't face the happy faces of my comrades inundated as they were with families and girlfriends, so I retreated moodily to my bed.

I had just dozed off when there was a crash at the barrack room door, followed by the stentorian bellow of Sergeant Bennet.

"Lance Corporal Wicks, stand by your bed!" And to my astonishment in strode Sergeant Bennet, but no longer a Sergeant, for he was now wearing the insignia on his forearm of a Company Sergeant Major. This was surprising enough, but the most amazing thing of all was that there, stood next to him, was the diminutive figure of my father.

I almost fell over with shock — I could not believe my eyes. My father, who if he had a shilling in his pocket, always gave it to us kids in preference to his own needs. I knew that he had no money and was always too proud to ask. How had he done it? My wonder only increased when I learned that he had bicycled all the way! My father in his mid-sixties, with a chest so bad that sometimes only willpower had kept him alive, had cycled all this way to see his second son receive his promotion. No longer did I feel envious of my mates and their families — I had a father to be proud of.

Dad had left the day before on his old bicycle, with his best suit, boots, razor and towel, clean shirt and two loaves of bread and a bottle of water, all packed into a clean sack tied over the handlebars. He had slept in an empty barn the night before and, upon reaching Woking, had changed and shaved in the public toilets.

As we were marching onto the sports field, I had half thought that I had caught a glimpse of a blue-clad figure, wheeling a bike through the spectators. No, it

66

could not be, I'd told myself, but I was wrong. Man! I was so proud. What man ever had a father like mine?

Tears rolled down my cheeks, embarrassing both of us as we hugged and slapped each other awkwardly on the back. The Sergeant Major turned away and strode out of the barrack room. It transpired that my father had remembered the name of my Drill Sergeant, and, after we had marched back to the barracks, he had asked for Sergeant Bennet.

There were several persons being presented with medals and other decorations by the General. The usher had pointed out Sergeant Bennet and afterwards took my father over to speak with him. The new Sergeant Major had been very impressed by my father, who, it has to be said, was wearing all his medals for the occasion, and took him to the Sergeant's Mess as his guest for a well-deserved meal.

He escorted us round the various displays. There were races between the Royal Mounted Military Police and the motorcycle team over a short distance, which amazingly, the horses won, scoring a complete whitewash. There was a display of police dogs, including one by a large Alsatian, who not only rode pillion on the back of his master's motorcycle, but leapt off whilst the vehicle was in motion and captured a running make-believe thief. There were demonstrations of dogs sniffing out explosives and drugs. There were also demonstrations of physical training, judo, basketball and a comic fancy dress football match. Sweating squads of men stripped down two motorcycles into their various component parts and then, dividing the parts between them, scaled a wall, a huge net, and crawled through big sewer pipes, before finally swimming across a large pool, to assemble the bike on the far side. The winners being whoever could fire it up and then do a complete circuit of the field carrying all members of the five aside team.

We viewed some of the more grisly exhibitions in the marquee of the Special Investigations Branch and watched a demonstration of parachuting. Military Police took part in a static military map reading exercise, which carried a small prize for the winner, and which, to my amazement, was won by my father.

Sergeant Major Bennet had a word with the Entertainments Officer, and my father was put up for the night in the Officer's Mess. When I saw Dad the following day, he looked slightly the worse for wear. It turned out that the Colonel, being a keen amateur gardener, had monopolised my father all evening, buying him several schooners of vintage sherry. As my father rarely drank, he was feeling somewhat out of sorts the following morning.

The Sergeant Major then sprang another surprise on us. He had been to see the Rail Traffic Warrant Officer and presented me with the rail warrants "Didcot to Littlemore via Oxford". I had been worrying about my father riding back, and was both relieved and grateful until I realised that they were from Didcot.

"That is not a problem," Sergeant Major Bennet replied. "I shall take you to Didcot myself. I have to go to the Reading Hospital to see my wife, and the Welfare

Officer has kindly loaned me a jeep from the motor pool."

He was as good as his word. The bike was slung on the back of the jeep, Dad rode in front, and I sat in the back, slightly encumbered by the bike, one kitbag, two suitcases and a bored Springer Spaniel. My father treated us to a great fish and chip meal, paid for by his winnings, and eventually we arrived at Didcot Station.

I took them both into the refreshment booth for a cup of tea, but to my surprise, the manageress refused to accept payment. Finally our train appeared, and Sergeant Major Bennet made his goodbyes and collected the dog from a group of admiring children who had been feeding him biscuits.

The bike was loaded into the guard's van, complete with my kitbag, and we embarked on the last leg home.

We arrived in the same way that I had left all those months before — Dad pushing his bike, with the kitbag balanced on the handlebars. Mother rushed down the garden path to greet me and almost suffocated me in the process.

I was home!

Home On Leave

I awoke back in my own bed to the smell of eggs and bacon. A few seconds later came the call of my mother.

"Peter — breakfast!"

I threw open the bedroom window whilst simultaneously struggling into my old dressing gown. I was amazed to find out how much it had shrunk, or more likely, how much I had grown.

It was a glorious morning. I could hear the solitary insistent "Dong! Dong!" of the Littlemore church bell calling the faithful to early morning communion. I had belonged to its church choir since I was seven years old, and I decided that I would go to the eleven o'clock morning service. I had successfully come through what was possibly the worst twenty-two weeks of my life, and I thought that it would be appropriate to offer a prayer of thanks.

I washed, dressed and ate my first home-cooked breakfast in months. Afterwards I went outside to get my beloved bicycle. Before leaving for training, I had carefully wrapped it in cardboard and greaseproof paper to protect it, and then hung it up in the beams of my father's shed out of the way. Imagine my shock to find that it no longer hung there. My little brother had availed himself of my absence and had taken the bicycle for himself. I finally found it, crushed under a disgustingly dirty rabbit hutch behind the shed and in a woeful condition. The beautiful frame was deeply scratched; bits of cardboard were stuffed into the wheel spokes to make a noise; the front wheel was buckled and both tyres were flat and split beyond repair. The beautiful Lucas dynamo set had been swapped for a pair of roller skates.

But what was the point of complaining? My mother, who could deny him nothing, had given him the bike to borrow until my return, on condition that he looked after it. My mother, who was nearly blind, but would not admit it, had been totally taken in by him, as usual. I contented myself by clipping him around the ear and prepared to walk to church.

There were lots of faces to greet me at church. Jack Hudson and his brother Les, Gordon Knight, Rosemary Clinkard, the Beckets — father and son, Bob Miller, the vicar Reverend C.C.L Buckwell, Mr Quelch the choir master and Mr Tanner who was now a sidesman, and many others — too many to mention. After church there was a wonderful surprise. Outside, waiting to greet me was Paula McGillick and her soon-to-be fiancé Michael Kelly and his brother Jim. These three went to the Roman Catholic Church, a couple of hundred yards down the road, and they had seen me going in.

I had a very good friend called Paula McGillick, she was an Irish girl. We met when travelling on the bus to Oxford. She was a very pretty girl too, with a lovely personality, she had come over from southern Ireland to join her father, who had a job in a car factory. She soon became very popular in my circle of friends, joining us in football and cricket.

I had had a very uneasy relationship with my sisters and she became a very good friend and confidant, more than they could be.

Most of my male friends were hopelessly attracted to her. One of her great talents was playing the piano, every few weeks or so my friends and I would be crammed into her front parlour gathered around her old piano with its couple of wonky notes, singing a collection of Irish songs in exaggerated Irish accents. On of my good friends, Mike Kelly, who was also Irish, was her boyfriend and later they were married. On her sixteenth birthday we held a party for her at her house and it was there that I had met Shelagh Bennett.

Shelagh was tall, slender and blonde, with a striking resemblance to the Hollywood actor Tony Curtis' wife, Janet Leigh. And although younger, the similarities were startling. I escorted her home that night and that was the start of a very strong relationship. We went everywhere together and I worshipped her, it was an innocent relationship, neither one of us knew the facts of life. This was common in the 1940s and I always envisioned that we might get married one day.

Mike and Paula had come to welcome me home on my first leave, but Shelagh was noticeable, for her absence.

Paula was distressed to hear that I had not received even one letter from Shelagh in all the time I had been away. Was she aware that I was home on leave? I did not think so. Paula offered to go over to Shelagh's house with Michael that same afternoon to see what the situation was.

It turned out that Shelagh had met someone else, and I was history. Paula and I cried together. I cried for myself, and she cried for me.

I felt as if my heart had been ripped out of me, and despite the surplus of would-be girlfriends, I had no enthusiasm for it.

I decided to visit my old school, Southfield Grammar School for boys, so one afternoon, a few days later, resplendent in my new uniform, I walked over. The school day had just finished when I walked through the gates. A few of my old classmates, now elevated to the upper sixth form and cramming for university, were still in attendance, and they greeted me with open arms.

I had badly wanted to go to university, but my parents' situation made this impossible, and I did not want to add to their burden. My mother had been upset when I decided to leave school and get a job, but I think she was also relieved that I would now contribute to the upkeep of the family. As we talked, several of my old teachers came out of the school gates, including my old form master, Mr Brashour and my English master, Doctor Freeboirn-Smith, a man who had been convinced that I would become a writer of books. It turned out that he was right, though it took nearly sixty years for me to put pen to paper.

We chatted happily for ten minutes or so, and then the headmaster, Mr D.G. Perry appeared. In all the five years I had spent at the school, the great man had never condescended to utter one word to me; I was the lowest of the low — a scholarship boy.

"Wicks is it?" he asked.

I was surprised that he even remembered my name.

I replied, "Yes, I am." I felt proud; I had achieved my first stripe.

Then, looking at me with contempt, he maliciously said, "Of course, you are really only a Private. That one stripe is just a make-believe rank! All your colleagues have obtained King's Commissions — is that all you could manage?"

I wished for the ground to swallow me up. I turned and headed blindly down Granville Road and out of the school gates for the very last time. I perceived that I would never walk into them again until I had done something of merit in my life. I have never returned or joined Southfield Old Boys Association. I had always felt like a pauper amongst princes, and that one moment, those few words had brought it all back.

The rest of my leave I spent helping my dad on his three allotments, or walking with Paula and Mike. They did their best to cheer me up, but it was almost with a sense of relief that I headed back to the army.

Fate had not finished with me, however. My mother had decided to iron my uniform. I was not allowed to wear civilian clothes in public, besides of which, it is doubtful my old clothes would have fitted me. As she was ironing my trousers, a knock came at the window — it was her neighbour with a bag of apples for her.

She turned her back to speak with Mr Hallett, as my sisters, Betty and Joyce, came into the room fighting over a skipping rope. My mother had left the electric iron sitting on our dining table, upon which she had placed the trousers.

Seconds later, the iron was flat on its face, having been knocked over in the argument, and was sizzling directly onto the uniform fabric. An enormous scorch mark was imprinted right across the seat of the trousers.

We spent all day trying to get the scorch mark out, and even tried rubbing it with a half-crown piece, but, although we did succeed in reducing the burn mark, it made the material as delicate as tissue paper. I did have an army greatcoat with me, and, when I went out, I was very careful to wear this to conceal the damage. The trouble was that that month was one of the hottest we had had for decades, and I almost collapsed from heat exhaustion.

The worst bit, however, was when I got back to barracks. When I reported my return to Inkerman Barracks guardroom, the greatcoat was peeled away, the damage was revealed, and I was arrested. My punishment was to be demoted for one month, all leave and privileges stopped, two hours of kitchen duty every night and extra drill Saturday and Sunday. I also had to buy a new uniform and cover the cost of the damaged uniform *and* pay for stores replacement, plus tailoring costs. Although only the trousers had been damaged, I also had to pay for the jackets.

What little money I received was stopped to pay the bill, and it took me 6 months to clear it. C.S.M. Bennet spoke up for me, but it was like they said — "Rules is rules!"

The Sea Crossing

One week later, I was posted. Several of my colleagues were posted to Northern Ireland, a cushy post at that time. Others went to Cairo, Egypt, or various locations in the United Kingdom. Some were sent to Malaya, which was then a hot spot, and for this they had to endure jungle training in the woods behind Inkerman Barracks for six weeks. The woods were full of non-venomous snakes, all imported for the purpose, and other creepy crawlies. The biggest posting was to Korea (I lost one of my school friends to that war; he was caught out by a booby trap). One of us was sent to Paris, and I, with some twenty others, was posted to Germany.

A week later, our little party had embarked upon the troop ship that ran a ferry service from Harwich to the Hook of Holland. We crossed at night. The ship was uncomfortably hot and stank of diesel. It was the first time I had actually seen sailors in army uniform, and I was surprised to find that the army actually ran boats and even aeroplanes.

It was October, and the crossing was rough. As this was a night crossing, we had all just been fed a greasy evening dinner of indigestible sausages, carrots as hard as bullets and a strange sort of reconstituted potato, masquerading as mash. Old hands, who had made the trip before, solemnly advised us to eat a hearty meal — for reasons no one seemed prepared to explain.

At 10p.m. we set sail — if that's what you'd call it! The boat seemed to travel crabwise in a series of sickening lurches across the tops of enormous waves. The wind shrieked and howled as we were catapulted down into one trough and up again, only to plunge into another. Everything vibrated, wires, steps, stanchions etc., to such an extent that it seemed the old ship would shake apart. It didn't help much when a rumour arose that one of the lifeboats had vanished.

Soon, we were fighting for space at the railing.

Rain hurtled down in sheets, and, now and again, a flash of lightening would enliven the proceedings. Some of us, me included, doubted that we would ever see dry land again.

We had a choice; those who had nothing left in their stomachs to bring back up could lay down on damp bunks, steaming like wet dogs, and pray for unconsciousness, or, if still wracked with nausea, we could stagger outside onto the main deck to be jolted, soaked and bashed about by a storm that was clearly enjoying itself. Feeling that I wanted to die, I crept into a top bunk and was soon unconscious.

I awoke just after dawn. Sunshine was streaming though a porthole level with my face, and the ship was steaming into harbour on a millpond surface as sedate as the River Thames.

Even as I focused, I caught my first glimpse of Holland. A battleship-grey post jutted out of the sea, and on top of it, a herring gull preened its feathers. I slithered down from the bunk and crawled out on to the deck.

During the night, my peaked cap had dropped onto the floor and someone had been neatly sick in it. I could not accuse anyone; for all I knew, it could have been me. I held it in the toilet bowl and pulled the lever. It worked well enough, but I almost lost the cap, the pressure was so great. Had it not been for the cap badge tangling with the chinstrap and jamming within the S bend, I would have lost it for sure.

I saw one of the army sailors coiling a large howser.

"Not a bad crossing," he called. "One of the smoothest we've had for a long time. Hungry? They do very good bacon, eggs and fried bread in the harbour canteen."

My reply was lost in my precipitate rush to the nearest guard rail.

An hour later, several hundred men in a vast variety of uniforms, were paraded in various groups on the jetty, whilst a roll call was made. There we waited, in a great pathetic steaming mass, to be led through the cavernous customs hall.

After a while, a military police lorry turned up, and, amidst the catcalls and boos of our disgruntled fellow passengers, we were taken to the little military police house. Here, we were allowed to shower, change into dry uniforms and drink hot, sweet tea or coffee before we were dosed with some green concoction.

By 9a.m., we were recovered and somewhat surprisingly, hungry. We were taken into the little mess room, where two attractive Dutch waitresses served us a lovely meal. There was gleaming white and silver chinaware, starched tablecloths and ivory handled cutlery. It was obvious that the meal had been carefully chosen — not a hint of grease in sight.

Germany

At 10a.m., our small party was driven to the railhead. There, before us, stood a gleaming brown and gold steam train. As befitting our new status, we were placed in the carriages marked "Officers and N.C.O.s only". Presumably, before the war, these had been first class carriages, and the white-coated Dutch steward assigned to us took great pride in telling us that these had once belonged to the Orient Express.

We travelled through a country so flat that I could scarcely believe what I was seeing. For mile upon mile, we thundered through the golden October sunshine, between russet fields. Cities stood out in the far distance like islands, but there was not a hill in sight.

At every rail crossing, there were hundreds of people on foot and on bicycles waiting patiently to cross. Girls in flowery skirts, young men, bronzed and golden haired, in pale blue dungarees, all chattering and waving as we went past.

Here and there stood a windmill with sails lazily turning. Upon the sail of one, a Union Jack fluttered in the breeze.

We passed a canal, where great, patient carthorses towed enormous flat-bottomed barges. The captain sat with his feet dangling inside the stern cockpit, puffing contentedly on a white clay pipe as he steered the enormous tiller, his wife on the middle deck pegging out clothes, which waved like bunting down either side of the vessel. The captain's wife, or "first mate", blew us a kiss as we passed, and the baby, in a little play pen behind her, waved his rattle. The captain's sons, or "crew", led the two great dray horses along the canal path, whilst a young woman, who could have been his daughter, rode a bicycle a few hundred yards ahead, presumably to warn anglers, of which there were many, of the barges' imminent approach. The train driver gave two toots on his whistle in acknowledgement.

We passed many white-painted houses, with their curiously "flap-eared" roofs, that reminded me of a legion of cocker spaniels, all sitting to attention.

The white-coated steward came through and informed us that we were in the first sitting for dinner, and we followed him into the immaculate dining room, where there were chefs with tall white hats and pretty waitresses who were in formal black dresses with starched white aprons, cuffs and collars.

There was no menu, but that was the only thing missing. The meal was a chef's delight. We ate with silver cutlery and gold banded china. I heard afterwards that the cutlery was carefully counted before the other ranks arrived, and both cutlery and china were replaced by basic N.A.A.F.I. eating irons and earthenware.

We came to the border town of Aachen, where the train stopped, and two German customs officials, resplendent in grey and green uniforms, climbed aboard. They walked through the train, checking the manifest lists and challenging various individuals in perfect English to open their bags. They were accompanied by two medium-sized spaniels, which passed amongst us, sniffing excitedly.

Whilst we were there, one of the spaniels, his tail wagging furiously, suddenly sat down in front of a sergeant from the tank regiment. The two officials immediately took him under arrest, and we did not see him again. I learnt afterwards that the dogs were used to sniff out marijuana and other drugs, and that the troop trains were a favourite method used by the drug smugglers to get drugs into Germany.

As we left Aachen, we saw lots of poles, each having a small platform fixed to it. These, we were informed, were for storks to nest upon as an alternative to their favourite nesting sites — chimneys. Quite a few people had died as a result of coal gases not being able to escape up the chimney when it was blocked by the birds. We saw many of the storks, which were so big that one wondered how such a large bird could perch without damage to the roof.

Eventually we steamed into Germany, which had a spectacular rolling countryside of lakes, farms, woods and villages. I was struck by the fact that there were few tractors about. I saw men in short-sleeved shirts with scythes, cutting hay, horses pulling goods wagons, and even a horse-drawn tram. On the main autobahns, great diesel juggernauts, towing as many as three trucks, thundered through the countryside.

I remember that we passed by what had been a main road bridge that had been bombed so precisely, that it was as if some giant hand had scooped out the centre, and left houses and a church totally unscarred.

At mid afternoon, we were called for coffee or tea if required — this time served in N.A.A.F.I. earthenware mugs. As we rolled through the countryside like lords, I was struck to see how few factories had survived — acres upon acres of skeletal, burnt-out factories, sheds and city centres. There was grey dust and rubble everywhere, and amidst it all were people toiling like ants. Every so often, a great, gleaming, ultra-modern building rose up through the devastation. Although I did not recognise it at the time, this was what politicians described as the rebirth of Germany.

Just as the streetlights were coming on, we arrived at our destination — Bielefeld. We disembarked, and the train pulled out. We were met by a military police sergeant, together with a German driver in a big scammer troop carrying lorry. Soon we were jolting through the busy cobbled streets, heading eastwards to the outskirts. Twenty minutes later, we had arrived in, what was then, a tiny village.

We travelled up a charming lane surrounded on all sides by apple tree orchards, and passed a pub (or café as they were called in Germany), where several older men in leather shorts toasted us with steins of lager, and a plump barmaid blew us a kiss.

Finally, we arrived at a picture postcard building, which was one storey high and had a thatched roof. It was surrounded by flat fields containing goats and horses, all grazing contentedly. We found out that the building had acted as the village school, but the children were now at a very large, modern school in the district, and that the council, with a sharp eye to business, had hired the empty building to the military police. It was ideal, inasmuch as it had four airy classrooms and an assembly hall, whilst the army had built a prefabricated cookhouse and dining room to the rear. Two of the classrooms had been turned into dormitories for our small party, whilst the assembly hall continued as a lecture room, and when the chairs were pushed back, as a gymnasium.

Original children's paintings still decorated the walls, and the children's toilets and basins were still in place — a drawback when many among our party were well over six feet tall.

This was to be our home for two weeks, and we spent our days wandering the sun-lit lanes, with occasional visits to the café and on one occasion to see Stewart Grainger in an English historical film at the local cinema. I was amazed to find that almost everybody, except the very old, spoke English, and this probably had to do with the fact that almost all films were from Hollywood, and of course English pop songs predominated.

Every morning, we sat through interminable lectures from old soldiers, mainly concerning sex, booze, fish and chips and precious little else. In the afternoon we were taken out, complete with sandwiches, on tours of the towns and points of interest.

Every night two of us would be called upon to man the office as per army regulations. It was the first time that I had ever worked through the night. We sat up in a small, comfortable office in the over-stuffed chintz easy chairs next to the telephone in case of emergencies, but it never rang in all the time we were there.

Sitting in front of a roaring log fire in what must have been the teacher's common room, with its thick Persian carpet and book-lined shelves, I discovered the *Wind in the Willows* by Kenneth Graham, and not having read it before, I sat enthralled by the adventures of Mole, Ratty, Badger and Mr Toad. I did two nights on night duty, in which time I managed to read the book from cover to cover.

On the second night we were there, we were all awoken by a resounding crash from the kitchen, and we all dashed out in our pyjamas. There, in the middle of the tiled floor, at three o'clock in the morning, stood a large goat with a basket round its horns. Pots, pans and two trays of cutlery were on the floor, as well as several half-eaten loaves of bread, which had been in the basket. It transpired that the door had a faulty latch, and the goat had formerly been the children's pet.

On the second Sunday, a small party of us were taken into Bielefeld to a small green-painted tin shed, which was a small chapel built by British prisoners during the last war, and now adopted by the British army of the Rhine.

We returned at 4p.m. for tea, and there, to my surprise were two M.P.s who had come to collect me. It turned out that they had escorted a military prisoner to the glasshouse (the nickname given to his majesty's military prison) at Bielefeld. Apparently, I was to join the strength of 102 Provost Company, based in Dusseldorf. The two Lance Corporals were staying the night, and I was to leave with them the following morning.

Monday morning, I had said goodbye to my former companions and was sat huddled up in my army greatcoat in the back seat of an open-topped jeep.

After three hours of fast travelling, we arrived at the outskirts of Dusseldorf, via the autobahn. My companions told me that, because the road had been laid in 21 foot stretches of concrete, each ridge of concrete would cause the tyres to clump, something similar to the rails of the old British railway line, with their hypnotic clickety clack. It further transpired that a great many accidents occurred when drivers travelling at high speed fell asleep at the wheel. On the way, I was regaled with macabre tales of crashes they had attended.

I was impressed by the magnificent town of Dusseldorf. Wonderful green copper-domed buildings fronted the splendid Rhine River, along with gleaming shop fronts, as elegant as anything in New York or London, beautiful parks and a magnificent wide boulevard named Konigsallec, all patrolled by elegant ladies stationed every twenty yards or so. It was some time before I realised that these were ladies of the night.

Great modern stores, including Woolworths and Macys, ranged either side of the boulevard with their flower gardens and ornamental fountains. There were elegant clothes shops, pavement cafés, art galleries and lighting shops, a magnificent railway station, all surrounded by glass and steel office blocks.

Trams clanked along the black-cobbled roads. Bells rang, cars hooted and parked across pavements, and people shopped, walked and chattered in one vast, heaving mass. Yet, just behind this front, the old commercial heart of the city was a bare wilderness; a huge plain of derelict earth, flattened by warplanes and now being dragged clean by huge crawler tractors and lines of lorries and carts.

Two things that struck me most were the young children doing cartwheels for pennies and the overpowering smell of cigars. It seemed that every able-bodied male in the town had a cigar permanently clamped between his teeth.

"Oompah" bands predominated, and every corner had its pavement artist or accordion player, often both. A clown on a unicycle handed out leaflets, and German policemen in old-fashioned black uniforms and strange leather helmets patrolled the streets.

Birds! There were birds everywhere! Mostly pigeons, strutting amidst the crowds of feet that threatened to crush them. At one point, I saw an old lady trundling along the pavement, chatting excitedly to her companion, a large French stick poking out of her heavy shopping bag, and perched there, unnoticed by the two ladies, was a grey town pigeon, contentedly pecking at the loaf.

It seemed that there were almost as many birds as people; great grey, white and blue birds, strutting across the roads in front of the fast moving traffic, and upon one tram clanging its way down the Konigs Allee, half a dozen pigeons were comfortably ensconced on its roof, like six old ladies taking a well earned rest.

102 Provost Company C.R.M.P. was situated in a residential district of Dusseldorf. The building was set in a leafy, middle-class district of substantial houses, directly behind a large Catholic girl's school on the road named Graf Adolf Strasse. The building itself was a long, honey-coloured building, obviously erected in the grounds of the small house in one corner of the plot. The story was that the building had been put up as a party raising venture by the local Communist party some two years before, and that they had been unable to make it pay. 102 Provost Company had taken it on a short lease on very advantageous terms.

The building was long, without decoration of any type, flat roofed and five floors high. There was a small yard at the back, where we kept our odd vehicles, and which directly backed on to the girl's netball courts of the adjoining school. The close proximity of so many teenage men and young girls must have been a nightmare for the several burly nuns trying to supervise their well-heeled charges. I remember one nun, a Sister Mary from Donaghdee, Ireland, had a demeanour and voice so fierce, that Hans, our interpreter, said that even the Gestapo backed down in front of her.

The house had been converted into workshops, in which several sign writers, an upholsterer, three seamstresses, a tailor and a cabinet-maker plied their trades. There were even three gleaming Volkswagen Beetle cars, complete with smartly uniformed German chauffeurs. I had not realised that the British army was responsible for rescuing the Volkswagen Car Company from the ashes, and these were impressive little cars.

There was a basement in the main building and this contained the boiler room, kitchens and storeroom, with the N.C.O.'s dining halls on the ground floor. Also on the ground floor, reached by several wide steps and a modern glass panelled door, were the offices of the Commanding Officer, Major Brook, the Regimental Sergeant, Major Causon, and the second in charge, Captain John Betty, a well-known motorcycle racer and motocross champion. Further along was the General Enquiry Office, manned by the Duty Sergeant and two Lance Corporals. Further down the polished, tiled corridor was the shared office of Lieutenant Bill Sykes and Second Lieutenant John Stokes, who coincidently had been a scholar at Magdalene College, Oxford and who lived less than a mile from my house.

At the furthest end of the building was a strong room, full of equipment racks, loaded with arms, ammunition, tents and other such items. This was the kingdom of Company Quartermaster Staff Sergeant Harrison, otherwise known as "Q". Here, he reigned supreme with his two Lance Corporal stores assistants. It was said that he did his training with the Inland Revenue. He was so tight, that if you required a new pencil, you had to produce the old stub and sign for it. Heaven help us if we lost anything, for we never heard the end of it.

On the opposite side were the Pay Office and Orderly room, manned by a Sergeant, two clerks and the very beautiful shorthand typists. Next to that was the office of the Anti-vice Squad, which premises was shared with the two German interpreters.

The next two floors were a series of two-roomed bedrooms. Originally, each unit had consisted of a bedroom and sitting room, each being connected by a single door. In the interests of economy, however, both rooms had been turned into bedrooms, each containing one single bed, wardrobe, bedside table, small writing desk and easy chair. The main staircase ran up through the centre of the building and adjoining it, on each bedroom floor, were washbasins, toilets, baths and showers in a communal block, and that old army favourite, the Army Equipment Blancoing Room.

On the top floor, to the right of the N.C.O.'s bar and stores, occupying one half of the building, was the recreation room, used for exercising and dances, and occasionally for a court martial. This floor was ruled over by "Hooch", the best known dog in the British army and the official Military Police mascot. Officially, he was a drug sniffer dog, and he had had some successes, but, he loved beer (with a definite preference to Pilsners Lager), and it had got the better of him. Faced with a cache of drugs or a pint of lager, he would go for the beer every time. When I arrived at the Company, Hooch must have been about seven years old. No one was sure of his history, but it seemed that he had been rescued from a battlefield as a very small puppy. With the exception of Q and the Alsatian next door, he was a friend to everybody. He was sixty parts Dashund, with the long nose and body of that breed, and forty per cent Bull Terrier. He lived with the barman in a basket behind the N.C.O.'s bar on the top floor of the building, and he was a familiar sight in the town, riding in the back of a military police jeep, with a little custom-made red cap on his head and a khaki dog coat sporting a Lance Corporal's stripe and a long service medal. He looked the part of a real police dog.

R. S. M. Causton

Regimental Sergeant Major Causon was the lynch pin upon which the whole company of almost one hundred men and officers revolved. A few years back, the BBC made the hugely popular *Dad's Army*, and in Captain Mainwaring, it was almost as if R.S.M. Causon had come back to life: The same build as the Captain, remarkably similar facial features and matching voice. I have often wondered if the creators of *Dad's Army* had met the R.S.M. during the war somewhere. As I say, the resemblance was amazing. The only difference was that he swore — boy, did he swear! It had grown into such a habit, that I do not think he was even aware of it.

His wife, however, in total contrast, was a graceful brunette, half a head taller than him. She dressed elegantly, was charming, (even to us minions) spoke beautiful English and would close her eyes and shudder fastidiously every time her husband swore.

On the day the toilet system blocked up, I overheard the R.S.M. tell our Commanding Officer, Major Brooks, that the lower toilets were ankle deep in manure. The men laughed when we heard Mrs Brooks, the C.O.'s wife, say to Mrs Causon, "My dear, can you not get him to say 'sewage'?"

"I only wish I could," came the reply. "It's taken me twenty-five years to get him to call it 'manure'."

The Sergeant Major had an encyclopaedic knowledge of army law.

"I was a barrack room lawyer," he said. "I proved to be such a thorn in the army's side that they had to promote me."

He did not suffer fools gladly, and it was generally admitted that his bark was not as bad as his bite. He was a scrupulously fair man, and as I discovered later, had immense personal courage, and when my beloved grandmother died suddenly, he was kindness itself. Our afternoons would often be enlivened by his shout of, "Where's that bloody Q?" And the Quartermaster Staff Sergeant would come running to his master's voice. The Sergeant Major ran what is called a "tight ship". 102 Provost Company was a very busy military police station indeed, and all of us were overworked and distinctly underpaid.

Major Brooks, our Commanding Officer, was a tall, well-built, smart man, with the studious air of an Oxford Don. He and his wife were so alike in demeanour and looks they could almost have been twins. Our C.O. had one overriding fascination, and that was life after death. He questioned me at length concerning my beliefs, and I discovered that most of my colleagues had received similar grillings. He was an agnostic, who was interested in all forms of religion. He could talk at length upon Sikh, Moslem, Lutheran, Buddhism, Roman Catholic, Shinto and Hinduism.

Rumour had it that he was studying for a degree in comparative religion.

Captain John Betty of the Gloucester Regiment was our Second in Command. I said from the Glousters, because all officers in the military police were all seconded from certain regiments. There was only one true military police officer, and that was the Depot Quartermaster. All other officers wore the rank and insignia of their mother regiments. Captain John Betty was a motorcycle champion. His personal transport was a B.S.A. Road Rocket, with unbelievable acceleration and road holding. I rode it once, and it scared me half to death.

The official strength of the company was 10 sections of ten men apiece, together with one Sergeant and one full Corporal. In practice, there were only seven sections due to staff shortages. One section was based at the Hook of Holland depot, mentioned previously. One was based in the town of Wuppertal. One section was based at Krefeld and a further section at Munchen Gladbach. The rest of us comprised one, two and three Headquarters Section. The outside sections were all commanded by a Sergeant, assisted by a full Corporal and an interpreter. Each section also had one army chef, who in turn had two civilian kitchen assistants/ waitresses, a maintenance man, two typists and a chauffeur with an olive green Volkswagen Beetle bearing army markings. Each policeman also had a motorcycle. The Sergeant had a jeep and the Corporal a 15CWT Bedford "Paddy-wagon" truck. There was also a small contingent of part time cleaners, gardeners and mechanics.

Headquarters Company had a similar set up, except that each Lance Corporal at Headquarters was responsible for no less than seven vehicles each. In my case, I was allocated six motorcycles and a jeep. Each vehicle was required to do a minimum of 70 miles a month.

I believe that the idea was that, should there be an escalation of problems, cold war wise, and because every National Service man had to serve five years with the Territorial Army, forces could be made up and fully prepared in a matter of a few days.

Overseeing this vast collection of vehicles was "Tiffy". He was a Polish man serving with the Royal Electrical and Mechanical Engineers. His name was so unpronounceable, I don't think I ever heard him called anything but "Tiffy". Incredibly though, he ruled his German assistants like a martinet. He was still only a Private, but heaven help the Sergeant or Corporal who provoked his lashing tongue. He was also Captain John Betty's chief racing mechanic. In his view, every army vehicle had to be mechanically perfect, and if it wasn't, why not? A small, intense-looking man, I never once saw him in anything but oily dungarees, hands and face liberally smeared with oil. When Tiffy said, "Jump!" we merely enquired, "How high?"

By contrast, the Company Quartermaster Sergeant, "Q", was a large man of some twenty stone, and like Tiffy took his duties seriously. He trusted nothing and no one. He was said to leave coins under mats in his stores to check to see if the cleaners were honest. If a Sergeant requested six items for his section, he would supply five. Thus, the R.S.M., irritated by the complaints of the Sergeants, would bellow down the corridor, "Where's that bloody Quartermaster?"

Q was also convinced that the way to promotion was dependent upon the amount of charges or misdemeanours he could prosecute against his fellow man.

Every day, two or three of us would be lined up outside the R.S.M.'s office on the flimsiest of charges. We would be double marched, with cap and belt off, into his small, overworked office, our boots thudding in double quick time. The R.S.M. would be wincing behind a pair of pince-nez glasses as each thud reverberated throughout the building. We were always found guilty, and the standard punishment was to be demoted to the ranks for two days. Basically, this entailed removing the stripes from our uniforms and then sewing them back on two days later, or getting the Company tailor to do it, who was charging a small fortune for the job.

Ultimately, someone had a brainwave — stick them back on with wallpaper paste, and guess what — it worked! Yes, it worked well, and for some weeks we marched about with our uniform stripes glued on with flour and water paste, made up for us by one of the waitresses.

Disaster soon struck, however. Some 50 of us, Officers and men, had to attend a large church parade for Remembrance Day at the B.A.O.R. church at the Rhine Centre, a massive showpiece park on the outskirts of Dusseldorf that had originally been erected by the Nazis as a tribute to Hitler. It had numerous playing fields and athletics tracks, concert hall, cinema, restaurants and a very modern church.

We were required to attend to the car parking of an enormous number of vehicles, both military and civilian. All went well until we were caught in a massive deluge of rain, at which point, to the amazement of the onlookers, the glue holding on our stripes dissolved, and they peeled away in a soggy, floury mess. We were undone!

There was no love lost between the R.S.M. and Q Harrison. Having had half his Company paraded in front of his desk, having had to cancel two days local leave when he had planned to celebrate his wedding anniversary, and after a tense interview with Colonel Bowers, the District Provost Marshall, he was most definitely not happy.

"Where's that bloody Q?" he bellowed. "On parade! Double quick march." And the portly Q heaved up to his office, enormous carpet-slipper shod feet flapping like two great paddles (he was excused boots), with his enormous stomach bouncing one way and his matching bum wobbling the other.

Our Chief Clerk, Sergeant John Forrest, had secretly been training our Company mascot for some time, and as Q shot past the Orderly office, Hooch barked at his heels in perfect timing — LEFT, RIGHT, LEFT, RIGHT!

Whilst we all roared with laughter, Q tried to kick Hooch away, but the dog promptly responded by snatching one of Q's slippers and haring off down the corridor with it. We subsequently found it dumped in a pile of coke. Hooch was truly a remarkable dog. One afternoon, however, tragedy struck. Hooch was sat in the back of the jeep, whilst the driver and his mate went to investigate a break-in at a local N.A.A.F.I. They were some time, and on their return, Hooch was gone. His lead had been unclipped.

The Company had broken up a dog fighting ring some months before, and these people were suspected, but of course there were no witnesses. Appeals were made in the local press for his safe return. Pilsners Lager Company offered a reward, and he was even given an appeal slot on B.A.O.R. Radio. All to no avail.

Three months passed, and still nothing happened. Then one day, the R.S.M. and his driver were sitting in a jeep, waiting at the traffic lights in one of the sleazier districts of the city, when a small body came hurtling across the road and shot into the jeep. It was Hooch, barking excitedly and wagging his tail so furiously, that he almost seemed in danger of taking off.

He was in a sorry state; his claws were broken, and he had lost over a third of his body weight, plus his smart coat and hat were gone. He had a length of twine tied tightly around his neck, which he'd obviously chewed, in order to escape. He was covered in bites and bruises and the theory was that he had been used as a punch bag to train illegal fighting dogs. The former dog fight gang was suspected, but nothing was ever proved. In time he recovered and became his lovely self once again.

★　★　★

The first duty I copped was to guard the motor transport garage. It was probably the least-liked duty we were given. The garage was sited on the other side of town, about 5 miles from the headquarters. The garage or "MT Lines" as it was called, was sited on the grounds of a huge hotel, which had been destroyed by fire; only the blackened skeleton still stood. We learned that a lot of people had died in the fire, and, situated as it was on the banks of the River Rhine, the place was an eerie sight, even in fine weather. At four o'clock in the morning, it was a very strange place to be; the river mist swirling around the orange halogen lamps in the compound, the screeching of banging doors and the loud creaks from the old building, together with the wind howling across the compound like a myriad lost voices.

Oddly enough, the compound itself, which, according to locals, had been an old Jewish cemetery, had not been touched by the fire. About 100 yards square, it was bounded by an old-stone, two-metre high wall, which still contained the mounts of plaques which had been torn from the walls, and in one corner, on its side, was the sculpture of a large dog. This appeared to be very old and probably weighed several tons. The area was completely concreted over, and it was probable that many old Jewish graves were still underneath. On the southern wall was a large prefabricated shed, and it was a regular occurrence for rats to chase across the roof girders in full sight of the unfortunate viewer beneath.

My shift was from 5p.m. Saturday night to 7a.m. on Sunday morning. In Tiffy's office and behind his desk, was a small fold-up camp bed, a flask of tea and, on the wall, a telephone. I was about halfway through a lurid paperback novel I had found on the desk, when the telephone rang — an insistent "BRR BRR" in the chill atmosphere of the office. I climbed off the camp bed and picked up the phone — there was nothing. All of a sudden, though, I heard the unearthly wailing of seagulls. I shouted like a fool down the receiver, but of an answer, there was nothing. I dropped the telephone receiver as if it was hot; I had never heard of seagulls flying about at night.

Apprehensively, I went to the door and looked out over the compound. Some thirty feet away, a huge bank of fog, fantastically lit by the overhead orange lamps. I looked to my left at the blackened skeleton structure, which stood out in the moonlit sky, where the stars were like frozen diamonds of light. Rising up out of the rolling bank and half way up the building, in what must have been one of the hotel corridors, was a nightmarish green blue glow that seemed to hover in the empty window space, and then it was gone. Incredibly, there was not a sound; certainly no seagulls wheeled and cried in the frozen air, no cars moved, no lights glimmered in the sleeping city, and I felt as if I was the last living being on the far edge of time.

I rang the B.A.O.R. switchboard, of which this telephone was an extension. A very irritable and sleepy operator answered. After a taut conversation, he advised me — (a) that no one could possibly have rung me without his knowledge and (b) to take more water with it! I told my colleagues about my experience, and

101

frankly they scoffed; the worst problem that anyone else had encountered was the discovery of a fat rat jammed into a teapot. Luckily, I was never asked to do the duty again.

I was questioned at length by our Commanding Officer about my experience, to which he listened intently, but made no comment.

Two days later, I had worse things to worry about. I was ordered to report to Colonel Bower's office. He was the District Provost Marshal and the head of all military police units in B.A.O.R. 4 District. His office was in the middle of a modern office block, and I was directed to the lift for the second floor. I jumped into the lift just as the doors were closing. There were already three occupants inside as I entered: a middle-aged man and two women. To my surprise, they also were headed for the office.

Eventually, I was called into the inner office and not only was the Colonel there, but also the District Chaplain. The Chaplain started the proceedings, and after saying a prayer for divine guidance, proceeded to lecture me on honour, morality and duty. I stood there totally bemused, but it was only when he told me that it was my duty to marry the lady, that the penny dropped.

"But this is impossible!" I cried desperately. "I cannot possibly be the father of anyone's baby — it is not me!"

The Colonel sighed, and, rising to his feet, crossed to the outer office. He opened the door and ushered in the three people I had seen in the lift. The man glared at me and rapped out an unpronounceable barrage of words that had the office typist in the outer room covering her ears. The other woman glared and looked accusingly at me, whilst the third woman was crying. I now saw that she was young and in the advanced stages of pregnancy.

To my intense relief, the situation was cleared up easily enough in the end; it turned out to be a case of mistaken identity. We had a sister company, the 2nd Infantry Division BOAR Provost Company, and somewhat amazingly, they also had a Peter Wicks. The army seemed incapable of differentiating between us, and this was to lead to a great deal of confusion in my army career.

The first month I was there, I spent all my working hours in the main office, stock taking in the Quarter Master's Stores, or attending lectures in the mess hall on map reading and forward planning, moriarty English civil law and even religious instruction. I also had to look after my motorcycles. By 5 o'clock, we were exhausted, but our day rarely ended there.

However, during my fifth week, I copped for town patrol duty with three other comrades. At 6.30 in the evening, we paraded into the main office, collected our pistols and paraded in front of the R.S.M.'s critical eye like self-conscious fashion models. The R.S.M. was acting duty officer that night.

We were driven to the centre of Dusseldorf and dropped off in various city locations, where we were given our beat instructions before being left to our own devices.

Because it was my first night, I was accompanied by Corporal Jacques, an old soldier of vast experience.

Our beat was down either side of the Koenigs Allee with its gleaming shop fronts and crowds of late-night shoppers. Kids were doing cartwheels in front of us, amiable drunken old soldiers thrusting forward through the crowds to shake our hands, and hordes of young urchins diving around us on skates, mapping our measured tread along the wide pavements. The prostitutes were the worst however, and we dreaded walking past them. They would be stationed every twenty-five yards along the pavement and took great delight in propositioning us — actions speaking louder than words.

My most abiding memory was of the two of us trying to walk steadily down the main street with an enormous German man, who must have been at least six feet six inches tall, draped around our necks. He was breathing whiskey fumes so strong, I was beginning to feel lightheaded.

What was amazing was that we met an awful lot of friendly old soldiers, claiming that they had only fought on the Eastern Front against the Russians. I remarked to Helmut Schmidt, our interpreter, how friendly everyone was, and he told me, quite seriously, that before the British came, people lived in a nightmare of fear and now they had been given a new lease of life.

Despatch Rider

Life continued pleasantly enough for several weeks, and then a bombshell dropped. As previously mentioned, military policemen were expected to be proficient drivers of either motorcycles or jeeps, which, by pure fluke, I was, having passed my driving test in a Bedford 15CWT truck. However, the aforementioned "other" Peter Wicks was a proficient motorcyclist, and here lay the problem. There had been several incidents of mistaken identity. There was such confusion that at one time the War Office insisted upon calling me "Wilkes" — army number notwithstanding.

Once again, they'd got us confused, and orders came through appointing me as the official dispatch rider to Embassies, outlying stations etc., a wonderful job, except for one small problem — I had only ridden a motorcycle once or twice previously, and that was only round a barrack square. I had never gone above second gear.

Frantic calls were made to the British Army of the Rhine local office, but it appeared that the army's mind was made up — official courier I was appointed to be, and official courier I was — there could be no argument.

Accordingly, after several fits and starts on a foggy November morning, I drove my unaccustomed motorcycle out of the main gate and to my first call; there were fourteen calls in all. My predecessor used to complete his run in less than five hours. I was grateful for the fog because few passersby would notice my predicament — a smart policeman on a highly polished motorcycle, screaming down the high-speed autobahn in second gear, at a mind boggling twenty-five miles per hour. Whenever I could, I practised changing gears up and down, until my left foot on the gear change lever was in danger of dropping off.

It took 15 hours to do that first day's run, but eventually after some six months, I was able to complete the run in four hours. I will never forget the excitement I felt when I crossed the 60mph barrier; the empty stretch of autobahn in front of me, dead straight for many miles, a keen wind at my back thrusting me down the shallow gradient, the road surface dividers clunk-clunking against my wheels. The heavy old motorbike flashed down the road at almost 80mph. I could almost visualize crowds cheering and a brass band playing, but all I got was an annoyed "CAW" from a disgruntled pair of crows, whose roadkill dinner I had interrupted.

All that winter, I persevered, and no one guessed my secret. By March I was thoroughly proficient in the handling of my machine, and motorcycling became a pleasure rather than a burden. I got to know the roads around Dusseldorf pretty well, and upon one occasion was overtaken by a gang of Birmingham Hells Angels on their way back to Holland. They were so delighted to see me, an English man, that I was practically dragged into a riders' café, where we all consumed copious amounts of Schnapps and Vodka. This resulted in me returning to the depot wearing the uniform of a Hells Angel, and with a German army helmet in place of the usual army crash helmet that I habitually wore. The upshot was that I had to apologise to the civilian staff for the upset I had caused by entering the kitchen in such a costume. I was also busted down to Private for seven days. Riding a motorcycle was not so much fun after all.

In the winter, there was no peak on the helmets to protect one's eyes from the driving rain, and the heavy motorcycle gauntlets we had to wear soaked up the rain like sponges. It became routine that every hour I would stop and let the engine idle for ten minutes, whilst I dried out the gloves on the exhaust pipe of the bike. The motorcycle great coats we were expected to wear were as stiff and unyielding as tank armour and almost as heavy. As for the army riding breeches . . . words fail me. Every time it rained, the breeches, which were already tight, would shrink, and they would shrink so much, I found it difficult to walk. Add to that the riding boots, tight to the calves and full of water, and woollen socks shredding themselves round the ankles, and you had an ensemble that was both uncomfortable and ridiculous, as-well as difficult to take off. It usually required two good friends to assist in tearing off the offending articles. The worst bit however was that the knees of the breeches had to be blanched white on the inside with white tennis shoe whitening cream.

Whenever it rained, it would leave both biker and motorcycle in pools of white shoe cleaner.

One day, whilst driving down an icy lane with a frozen stream running alongside, my feet down to maintain balance, I came across a crowd of people all skating or sliding on the hard ice surface. I was greeted with much mirth and enthusiasm. It turned out to be some sort of feast day being celebrated with nuns and clowns on ice. There were school children in fancy dress costume, and the town's silver band accompanying them for all they were worth. The mayor was there, together with his corporation. There were sledges, wine barrels, hot chestnuts and even a quartet of leather-trousered, back-slapping German dancers.

A very pretty, laughing Rhine maiden flagged me down, and I was led to meet the mayor. Coincidently, it transpired that his daughter was a doctor at the Radcliffe Hospital in Oxford, the very hospital in which I was born.

An hour later, having received some very extravagant hospitality, I was on my way.

One late November day found me riding back to H.Q. The temperature was in the minus degrees, the winds were buffeting the old motorbike, and the handlebars seemed to have taken on a life of their own. Several times, I rode perilously close to a ditch. Despite the minus degrees of cold. I found myself sweating under my heavy despatch rider's great coat. To make matters worse, I was travelling over bare heathland, without a tree or a bush in sight, and I was desperate for a pee; if I could have ridden the bike cross-legged, I would have done.

Then it started to rain. I would have gone by the side of the road, but there was too much traffic streaming past, and my clothes were highly visible. I gritted my teeth and rode desperately on.

At length, I came across a tall stone wall behind which was a steep sugar loaf shaped hill. A row of dark, forbidding trees led up to a steep path flanking a gravelled roadway. The wind howled through the treetops like a wild animal, and the trees themselves bowed and genuflected like living dancers trying to lift their toes up out of the sticky mud.

I pushed the bike behind the wall, and then realised that I could still be seen from the road. I looked into the embrace of the clutching trees, then I gritted my teeth and trudged on up until I came upon the brow of the hill. There was almost a full moon, and the grass leapt and dashed against the knoll like a silver grey sea of pounding waves. I looked down onto a most curious building. I had once seen a building like this in West Wycombe, Bucks; a part of the notorious Hell Fire Caves. As far as I could tell, this building was no more than a wall of arches set in a hexagonal shape and approximately some 60 ft in diameter. There were many monuments around the walls. Obviously the building was many years old and had been in use as a graveyard for some considerable time.

Even as I looked, there came, borne upon gusts of wind, the awful stuff of nightmares, a sound so familiar to my youth, a voice of hate, so malignant, that for a second or two I was paralysed with fear — it was the voice of Hitler!

And then something struck me on the helmet — a smooth round pebble from a slingshot. This was followed by another, which hit my goggles, somehow missing the lens, but breaking the metal nosepiece. Several other stones thudded into my body, the heavy great coat absorbing the impact. Through streaming eyes, I saw them; about a dozen black-clad figures coming out from behind the monuments. Several carried slingshots, the rest appeared to be carrying crude clubs. All were advancing upon me, their intention obvious. My fear suddenly vanished. I heard the panting voice of hysteria, with its message of hate towards the Jews. I thought of my school friend, Neville. I had been there when his parents had received the news that his grandparents, cousins and aunt had all perished in Auschwitz Concentration Camp.

A blind, unreasoning fury overtook me. I had a lightweight Sten gun slung across my shoulders which I was taking back to the armoury for repair as the cartridge clip was jammed onto the gun. Because to all intents and purposes the gun was still live, it had been unusually decided to return the gun with me. I also had my trusty old six shooter with me, and I now drew it; but it was all a bluff. We were not allowed to carry bullets, and, since an article revealing as much had appeared in one of the so-called newspapers of the day, they most likely knew that we were not allowed to carry ammunition, let alone fire a gun without having filled in forms in duplicate, triplicate and most likely in quadruplicate as well, it meant that I was a sitting duck.

As they got closer, I saw that most of the group were wearing some sort of black uniform consisting of flat leather caps and American style black army boots over black overalls. I had heard of such groups before, but had never seen one. These were the self-styled guerrillas of the Third Reich — Hitler's werewolves.

I noticed that a tall dandified creature wearing a black opera cloak with scarlet interior and a large swastika armband seemed to be leading the attack. I waved my pistol threateningly, which seemed to stop them for a moment, and then seeing that I was not in a position to fire, they crept forward again.

I reached behind me and took off the Sten, and then using the classic firing position, I waved them forward.

It was at that moment that a rock caught me across the head, and I fell to one knee, jolting the Sten gun, which sprayed forth its lethal hail of bullets. I saw the leader go down with a shriek of agony (he had taken two bullets to the leg), and the rest of the figures ran.

I performed what first aid I could then dragged him over to a pillar set centrally in the graveyard and forced his arms around the base, securing him with my handcuffs; it was my intention to leave him until he could be picked up. I then realised that I still needed to pee! The phonograph was still pouring out its message of hate, and so I decided to relieve myself on it whilst in full view of my enemy.

So much for the best laid plans of mice and men. What I did not see in time was the live cable powering the phonograph. There was a flash, and I felt as if I had been kicked in the stomach, such was the force of the electrical shock I had generated. I staggered back to my bike, leaving my prisoner crying piteously.

The trouble was that I had lost my bearings, and it was two days later before a German police patrol found the scene of the incident. The prisoner and my handcuffs were gone; his friends must have sawn through the handcuffs to release him.

All was not lost, however, for two days later, he was picked up in a local hospital with a shattered leg. They told me that he had blubbered like a baby. He was one of the nastier pieces of Nazidom, and he lost no time in giving up his fellow gang members. As far as I know, he died in prison.

Dress Rehearsal

The following spring we had a visit from Governor Dwight D. Eisenhower himself. This was of course before he became President of the U.S.A., when he was still our Supreme Allied Armies Commander. It was decided that 102 Provost Company, in other words us, were to form the guard of honour at the airport.

It was probably the worst decision ever made — we were hopeless! Why we had been chosen and not the Irish Guards or the Black Watch was a mystery to me. Some of my colleagues had not stamped on a parade ground in several years. True, we looked smart, but as for drill — we were like broken puppets.

We had just two weeks to learn the routine. Those of us who had recently come from the Depot were not too bad, but I'm sorry to report that Sergeant Major Causon, (who was probably at the time the Army's most efficient policeman) was as hopeless a drill instructor as could ever be found in the British army.

Sergeant Major Causon was a proud man, and, like so many old soldiers, he had been drafted into the army during the Second World War. For years, he had been a village constable, with little or no need for parade-style duties, but such was the need for military policemen, he had been fast-tracked into a position of great responsibility. Then, when the war ended, he had opted to remain with the corps. The problem was that his training in parade drill had been overlooked.

The Sergeant Major took up his stance at the head of the parade, and he certainly looked impressive. He shouted a command. The command should have been:

"PARADE BY THE LEFT — QUICK MARCH!"

But whether he was suffering from stage or parade fright, the command rang out:

"PARADE BEST FOOT FORWARD — MARCH!"

There was chaos. Several soldiers, totally baffled as to which was their best foot, stopped still, other marchers cannoned into them, with the result that several were buffeted over the pavement.

Hooch tore himself from his master's grasp and laid into his mortal enemy, the Alsatian from over the road.

The old German Servicemen, who lived in a hostel directly opposite, laughed almost fit to burst. Relations with them were friendly enough; in fact, at least half a dozen of them were found sitting upon the low wall opposite, playing cards or chess with noisy good humour whilst drinking copious amounts of home-brewed beer, which was so strong that even our dog Hooch couldn't stomach it.

The Sergeant Major, face as red as a beetroot, shouted, "COLUMN ABOUT FACE!" Which was a command totally unknown in the British Army. I shouldn't wonder if it wasn't a direct result of watching a Colonel Custer American Army film. As a result, some turned about to the left and stumbled, because the order had been given forcing them to turn on the wrong foot. Many of them stood stock still, whilst their comrades at the rear, who had not heard the order, ploughed resolutely on until the Sergeant Major was backed against a high strong wall.

It was probably unfortunate that this was the time of day when hordes of young mothers passed our building to collect their offspring from the infant's school just up the road. Word swiftly got around that something was going on, and suddenly we were besieged by hordes of onlookers. It was pandemonium! Children ran unrestrained around and among us, and at least one old soldier laughed so heartily we had to call an ambulance, fearing that he had had a heart attack.

For three days, we went through the hideous embarrassment of parading in front of our neighbours, and then, on the fourth day, it rained.

We were all congregated in the junior dining room when the Church Army mobile canteen appeared outside our front door. Twice a day we were visited by the refreshment van belonging to the English Church Army, which was a similar organisation to the Salvation Army, run by a Major and two lady helpers. Whilst he was in the hall serving out buns, shoe laces and razorblades, someone asked him how he was doing with the Church Lads Brigade. He ran a very impressive and popular band of church lads' volunteers, who had a first class brass band and were made up of a mixture of sons from the married family army estate and some German boys. I had seen them on several occasions at their church parades at the Rhine Centre, and they were impressive. Their average age was only about fourteen, but they could put a formation of guards to shame.

The problem was presented to the Reverend Major (I forget his name). He came up with a stunning formation. Five N.C.O.s were chosen (of which I was not one), and these were interspersed along the length of the column. There were to be six manoeuvres, each to be preceded by a blast from a whistle. Orders were to be whispered down the ranks and on one whistle blast from a chosen soldier in the ranks, the whole formation would turn, advance and check with perfect military precision.

It worked! That afternoon we paraded again, and to the astonishment of the old soldiers, put in a perfect performance full of confidence.

The next day we marshalled again. The trouble was that one old soldier had spotted our ploy and introduced his own whistle into the proceedings, blowing with marked abandonment, causing us to halt, stumble and stop until we felt dizzy.

There was another problem. When the assembled company came to attention, it sounded like a rattle of machine gun fire. The Reverend Major was consulted again.

"Does anyone play a drum?" he asked. I told him I could, so a side drum was borrowed from the Boy's Brigade and camouflaged by a 102 Provost Company sign to cover its original logo. I practised drumming so hard that my colleagues were volunteering for extra duties to get away from the noise, but it worked. Because he could no longer sabotage us, our whistle blower gave up in disgust. We still blew our whistles, but these were now enveloped by the sound of a drum roll from my furiously bashed drum.

It was then that our saboteurs pulled another stunt to upset our equilibrium. Three of the old soldiers came goose-stepping down the pavement in front of us dressed in their old army uniforms for the benefit of the laughing crowd. With uniforms tightly stretched at the seams, they goose-stepped daintily as a duck at first waddle. All their uniforms were old and obviously made for men much thinner in a previous life. They looked ridiculous as they smirked at their audience.

We were nonplussed, then someone suddenly started impersonating geese with a loud, "HONK, HONK, HONK!", and as one man, we all joined in. The ladies mainly clapped and cheered, and some even joined in with the honking chorus, as did the three old German soldiers we used to call Laurel, Hardy and Kaiser Bill, for want of their real names.

Laurel was tall and very thin, whilst Hardy was so small and fat that the kids called him Humpty Dumpty or Mister Egg. Kaiser Bill, named because of his drooping walrus moustache had a pronounced wobble, and looked as if he was about to burst into tears at the drop of a hat. All three of them were as tight as frogs (born out by the empty bottles on the opposite pavement), and to great applause from the watching crowd, the trio joined in and goose-stepped as delicately as a set of overweight chorus boys.

It was a shame that on the same side of the road, but hidden from the rest of us, appeared a young lady pushing a toddler in a pushchair, accompanied by her small toy poodle bitch. Behind her came Hooch's sworn enemy, showing a marked interest in what Hooch considered to be his girlfriend. With a throaty growl, Hooch hurtled towards his enemy, with his lead streaming behind him; unfortunately, as Laurel goose-stepped past Hooch, his delicately pointed toe caught in the dog's lead. Somehow or other, Laurel pivoted on one foot, spun and kicked Hardy in the stomach, before collapsing in front of him.

Hardy went down over Laurel like a felled ox, whilst Kaiser Bill, who was obviously in an alcoholic daze, sat down upon the pavement and proceeded to take his boots off.

Meanwhile, the dog fight continued apace with neither gaining the upper paw, until both were booted back by their irate keepers. The poodle eyed the combatants disdainfully and proceeded upon her way. When Hooch swaggered up to her, as befits a champion, she bit him hard on the ear.

Further revelations were to follow when Hardy was unceremoniously yanked to his feet. It proved that his too-tight uniform had given up the unequal struggle with his voluptuous curves and split down his spine from shoulder blades to builder's bum and beyond. Upon rising, it could be seen that his whole back was tattooed in glorious colour with a fox hunt in full cry and the fox disappearing with only his tail visible.

That night, peace was declared between us and the old soldiers, and they all came over with their carers to what is termed in army parlance "a glorious peace op".

The Inspection

At last, the great day dawned. The tailor and his assistants had worked overtime to smarten up our Sunday best, and we were now on our way to the airport in a big military troop carrier. It promised to be a hot day; the sun shone, and, stiff as tailors' dummies in our uniforms, we sweltered.

Eventually, we drew up in ranks of three in front of the red carpet laid down where the plane was to land. The carpet, though impressively long was of a lightweight, flexible material, and was clearly unsuitable for the purpose, for now a warm breeze had sprung up and begun to ruffle the edges of the said carpet.

Dust started to blow around us, and our newly whitened webbing belts, holsters and straps were looking decidedly grubby. We tried to protect the gleam of our highly polished toe caps by rubbing them on the calves of our trousers, so that we must have looked like a gaggle of flamingos.

After some minutes, the plane landed, and just as the fuselage door opened, the carpet developed a life of its own and flapped gently down the runway, with several airport staff in hot pursuit (we heard that pieces of it were found on the autobahn several days later).

From the plane poured a solid phalanx of soldier bodyguards, all above average height and completely obscuring the smaller General Eisenhower. The assembled "brass" took a chance upon which section of bodyguards the General might be surrounded by and led their parties in determined forays through the human forest, in order to shake the great man's hand.

The General swept by us like a dose of salts, straight into the reception hall. It transpired that there had been a threat upon his life and his bodyguards were taking no chances. All that work we had put in with whistles and drums was for nothing. Just to show that we could do it, we did a quick demonstration of our newly acquired skills for the benefit of the main onlookers and then we headed for the nearest bar.

One week later, a bombshell was dropped which made up for our disappointment at the airport. We were informed that we had been chosen for a snap inspection and stock take. The following morning, two enormous American automobiles arrived at our front gate and disgorged a dozen very smart and keen-looking American officers, complete with briefcases and slide rules.

To say that we were caught on the hop is no understatement. The duty Sergeant was sitting shirt-sleeved and braced at his desk behind a high fence barrier in the outer office, reading the *Daily Mirror*, whilst Hooch snored peacefully in a basket at his feet, when the officers burst in.

Sergeant Matthews leapt hastily to his feet, knocking his mug of tea all over his newspaper, whilst stubbing out his cigarette on the "no smoking" sign prominently affixed to his desk.

It seemed that all these officers were specialist officers in their own right. We learned afterwards that the officer who inspected the fabric of the building and the Quartermaster's Stores had in his previous working life been the manager of a large hotel.

The Sergeant Major, who had been planning a day off, arrived unshaven, and a keen observer would have been able to see that he still had his pyjama jacket on underneath his battledress blouse.

We were awakened by the strident clangour of the fire alarm and struggled bleary eyed outside to the back yard, where we stood shivering in a strange assortment of sleep attire.

A roll call was taken, and then we were all sent back to our rooms to change; there would be no breakfast that morning. All our kit had to be laid out for inspection on our beds, and these were critically assessed by the keen-eyed American officer. Afterwards, all available personnel, other than those on office or night duty, were ordered to the garages for a motorcycle and jeep inspection.

We duly paraded up to the old burnt-out hotel on the banks of the Rhine, where we were split into sections of ten apiece, with one of the American examiners allocated to each group.

As I may have mentioned, we had enough vehicles for four times our size, all of which had to be kept in perfect running order. First of all we were requested to start up all the bikes. Tiffy first poured a thimbleful of some mysterious liquid into each tank; he called it his elixir. Whatever it was, the engines exploded into life with just one kick. This was surprising, because the engines were normally very difficult to start, sometimes taking several minutes to tick over sweetly. The American officers were impressed, and when we knew the secret, so were we, for Tiffy had poured a thimbleful of whisky into each empty tank before topping up with petrol.

We were quizzed individually upon each of the machines under our care. Vehicles were inspected critically by each officer, who had a big check list. Drivers sweated under the bonnets, and even the undersides of the jeeps were checked. In some cases the wheels had to be removed to inspect the brakes.

We had a special section containing the highly polished jeeps, complete with sirens. These were used for motorcade escort duties only. Olive green, with gleaming brass accessories, they sported very powerful sirens, flashing lights and loudspeakers. Next to them stood my Embassy bike which had only just been delivered.

Up to this time, all the army motorbikes had been B.S.A. 500cc side-valve motorcycles, which were slow and ponderous with girder forks. The matchless 3 GL had only just been introduced into the British army, and I was one of the first to ride one on duty. It was a dream machine; lighter and smaller than the old B.S.A. bikes. The 3 GL was equipped with the new telescopic front forks, which made for a more comfortable ride. Although its engine was only 350 cc in capacity, it could leave much larger bikes standing, both in top speed and acceleration. The Americans were most impressed, and one even rode it around the yard.

It was after that that the bombshell dropped; we were all told to produce our driving licences for inspection. Not a problem you might think, except that I did not have one! It was humiliating when I had to explain that I had never been issued with one and had not even been on a course — the whole sorry saga was trotted out. There was an anxious, high-level conference, and the result was that I was issued with a licence on the spot, signed by the General himself.

Even Hooch, that sagacious dog, proved he was no ornament by leading one of the officers to a corner of the yard, where four dead rats were laid neatly side by side.

The following day, Hooch was promoted to Corporal, although he was not as impressed by the extra stripe as by the beer ration.

Petra — A Damsel in Distress

Early October found me and Ken Stone travelling along on the autobahn in Ken's jeep. It was about ten o'clock at night, and the fog was so thick that the visibility was down to a mere ten feet. I sat frozen upon the flat bonnet of the jeep, like some old ship's figurehead, trying to guide Ken with some very original hand signals in an effort to keep the vehicle on the road. I had never seen fog so thick. Not even the London pea-soupers could compete with fog like this; it was a complete white out.

We were on our way back home, having been out to take statements following a particularly nasty accident — a battle tank had pulled out during the night and crushed a tent full of German service organization personnel. We ourselves were not called out until two days later, by which time we could do little more than take statements from witnesses, and there were not too many of those.

Anyway, there we were, freezing to bits in a vehicle with no heater and only a canvas roof, travelling along the autobahn at a mind-boggling five miles an hour, sometimes drifting towards the left hand verge and, at other times, the right hand verge. Occasionally, great German lorries would thunder past us, festooned with

124

arc lights rather like ships in the night. But for the last half hour or so, there had been nothing.

Then, suddenly, a shape loomed out of the haze before us. Ken swore and stamped on his brakes causing me to slide off the bonnet. We were scared out of our minds; the autobahn at night is a pretty spooky place, and to see this ghostly shape materialise, having just interviewed the survivors of the tank accident, sparked our imaginations and shook us up, to say the least.

We clung to each other in terror for a brief moment, before common sense prevailed. What our weary and edgy minds had viewed as a ghostly shape, turned out to be an old eiderdown. A closer look revealed two small pairs of feet.

I walked round to the other side to investigate, and there, underneath the eiderdown, were two small figures — a young woman around twenty years old and a little girl about six years old. My first impression of them was of two frightened pairs of eyes. Both were dressed in rather curious clothing that had obviously been made for a much older woman and had been inexpertly tailored to meet their needs. The woman was dark skinned, presumably from a life on the land, and the girl, who was barefoot, was shivering uncontrollably. As I came towards them, the woman pushed the girl behind her and produced a large knife.

She was obviously terrified and wild, like an animal; it took a great deal of persuasion to get both of them into the jeep. The little girl was like a zombie, and all the time she was with us, I didn't hear her utter a single word. Anyway, we clad them in our uniform great coats and took them to the Salvation Army hostel to see the Reverend in charge.

The pair were extremely anxious throughout the journey and the woman clung to her knife, waving it threateningly in our direction every three of four minutes. We were intensely relieved to deposit them in the Salvation Army's care. We said our goodbyes and headed back to our depot.

We had a typist called Elsie, a beautiful girl, very religious and moral, and she was walking out with a Salvation Army Major. It was she who told us what had happed after we left the hostel.

The woman had taken a meal there and then abruptly run away, taking the girl with her. They hunted high and low for her and eventually found her hiding in one of the big wheely bins. It was a worrying period, as it was apparent that the little girl had contracted pneumonia. The woman was persuaded to leave her daughter in the good hands of the Salvation Army whilst she took on a small part-time job waitressing to support them both. As far as we were concerned, that was the end of it for us, but then Elsie told me a remarkable story.

The woman's name was Petra. She was of Dutch descent and had been a member of the Communist Party. The German Nazis had taken her family and transported them as slaves to East Germany, where, as a girl of barely sixteen, she had been grossly mistreated. She had been put to work on a farm owned by a local Nazi official, where she was kept in a stable by the man and forced to eat pig swill from the trough. He had taken great delight in tormenting her and had raped her daily, so that she soon found herself with child. His wife had hated the girl and covered her in cigarette burns.

In due course, the baby was born, and he placed her in an orphanage. For four more years, Petra continued to suffer, but she clung to one great hope — that she would be re-united with her daughter.

In time, the child was given to a prominent German family to be brought up as their own daughter, but Petra was determined to get the child back.

In 1944, the Russians entered the area, and the farmer's wife, who had so badly mistreated Petra, came to her, begging for protection from the Red Army, who it was said were doing dreadful things to Nazi women. The farmer had vanished, leaving his wife to face the music alone.

Petra took his shotgun and marched the wife into the stall where she had lived for so long. She tied her hands behind her back, stood her in the pig trough and then placed a noose around her neck before tying it around an overhead rafter, forcing her to stand for many hours. Then as a final gesture, she stabbed her in the leg with a carving knife and left her in agony.

Petra packed a small suitcase with the Nazi couples' valuables, grabbed what clothing she could find and fled. She knew where the orphanage was because her master often collected pig swill from there. But when she got there, it was empty and deserted — the occupants having fled.

Beds and furniture were still intact, although much of the furniture had been turned upside down by the Russian troops looking for loot.

The office was also still intact, although anything of value, such as typewriters, had been taken. The filing cabinet had been forced open, and many of its papers destroyed, but wonder of wonders — lying half-burnt in the grate, was the register of the people who had adopted the children, and even their addresses.

Whilst she was searching the papers, she heard a noise behind her. Turning she found a Russian soldier with a Tommy gun pointed straight at her.

Petra was led in front of a Russian official and despite her protestations that she was not a German, was put in a hard labour camp for 12 months, where she was given a hard time by the other prisoners. It was during this time that she acquired the knife for protection, and it soon became apparent that she was prepared to use it without compunction.

At the end of the 12 months, she was shown the gate. Returning to where she had carefully hidden her suitcase, she was overjoyed to find it still intact. The next thing was to locate her daughter.

Careful enquiries elicited the information that the would-be foster parents had been tied up to the railings in front of the house and burnt to death. Whilst she was combing the ruins of East Berlin, she came across small bands of feral children, who lived among the ruins.

Then she saw her — her daughter! She had not the smallest doubt it was her; there were certain physical similarities and defects which proved to her that this really was her child.

There was now the problem of getting the child back to her. A fourteen-year-old boy whose range of survival skills was limited led the little gang of waifs and strays. A short confrontation and the production of the knife convinced him to hand over the reins of leadership to Petra. He was fed up with the responsibility of leadership anyhow and stepped down to become her second-in-command.

Under her leadership, the group soon prospered. In fact they became feared among the citizens of East Berlin. The little gang had now grown to fifty, and Petra became their modern day Fagin. They survived by using their criminal skills: shoplifting, mugging, intimidation, and any other criminal activity that would bring in money to the small group.

The headquarters was a large cellar in a bombed-out site. Although the group prospered, Petra's daughter was still unable to speak; it was believed that she was traumatised by the brutal deaths of her adoptive parents.

Some eighteen months into Petra's leadership, one of the children came to her and told her that one of the "creepos", as they called the Communist Police, had taken one of the girls into his hut and was attempting to rape her.

Petra burst through the door and told the child to run — which she did. The man's lascivious attentions were now focused on her, and, being much larger and stronger than her, he managed to get behind her. She

129

bent forward, and as she did so, took the knife out of her boot and, stabbing upwards behind her legs, succeeded in castrating him.

Obviously the "creepos'" would now be after her, so she decided to leave Berlin, leaving her second-in-command in charge.

The first problem was to get out of the Russian zone, which she succeeded in doing by crawling with others under a mass of barbed wire fencing.

Once she and her daughter were safe in West Berlin, she had hunted for transport to take her into the western zone. A Swiss lorry driver was found who, for an extortionate sum, was prepared to take both her and her daughter through to Amsterdam.

Accordingly, she and her daughter rode in the high cab for many hundreds of miles. In the cab was an old eiderdown, which the driver normally draped over the engine to keep it warm. Petra and her daughter wrapped themselves in it in one corner of the cab and slept during the drive.

Shortly before we had met her, the Swiss driver had tried to force himself on her. Fighting back, she had produced the knife and stabbed him in the arm. With blood pouring from his wound, he had literally kicked her out of the cab and onto the concrete, before driving off with both her possessions and her beloved daughter.

About two miles further on, he had pushed the child out and, in a fit of remorse, had left the eiderdown on the road with her. Neither Petra nor her daughter had shoes, and all their money and possessions had gone with the lorry driver. It was in this predicament that we had found them — cold, hungry, wet and shoeless.

Although Petra lived in mortal fear of Germans, our typist, Elsa, succeeded in taking her under her wing, and the couple settled down to a spell of relative happiness. Petra had her job in the hostel as a waitress and kitchen hand, and Elsa, who was a dab hand with a sewing machine, produced many fine clothes for the pair of them.

The little girl soon began to speak, and it was some twelve months later that we heard that Elsa had managed to secure them a train fare to Amsterdam, and that she had later received a letter from Petra to say that she had found her grandmother, although her parents were long since dead.

We had a Sergeant, Sgt. Barnum (not his real name), and he was a crook. Every soldier in B.A.O.R. was allowed to purchase, for his personal use, 200 cigarettes at a much reduced price — literally for pennies. The good Sergeant was in charge of allocating duties to us poor mortals, and we soon discovered that by allocating our cigarette ration to him, we could avoid some of the more onerous duties that we could be saddled with.

British cigarettes commanded a high price in Germany, and he ran such an extensive operation, that he saved all of his pay and purchased two Mercedes Benz taxis, which he operated with civilian drivers all over Dusseldorf.

And that wasn't the only scam he had going. Once a week, he travelled down on the troop train to the Hook of Holland port with our interpreter, his partner in crime. The scam was small but inventive and brought them in a great deal of money. Helmot, our interpreter, would walk the length of the train offering packets of pornographic playing cards to the squaddies going on leave, knowing they would have money to burn. The Sergeant, passing as a civilian worker dressed in mufti, would follow at a discreet distance and make a careful note of all the purchasers.

At the port, he would reappear in full Military Police rig and arrest all those who had purchased the pictures. The purchasers, who had already spent an expensive sum, now found that the pictures were confiscated and were given the choice of either being arrested, with all the scandal that that would involve, or paying an exorbitant price to the Sergeant to avoid prosecution.

The whole process was repeated on the way back, resulting in the two men amassing enough money to start a dubious nightclub in Dusseldorf, which was nicknamed the "Snake Pit". Both men ran this scam quite happily, without fear of detection, for months . . . until they got greedy.

As each passenger embarked for the night sea crossing, they were issued with three blankets: two grey and one blue. In the corner of each blue blanket, the scammers, along with the issuing store man, burnt a cigarette hole on the edge, so as to be almost invisible and detectable only to a very keen eye. Non-smokers were annoyed to find that they were being charged for causing fire damage to the blankets, but they could escape prosecution by donating a sizeable contribution in the "Barnum Friends Society's" collection tin. All such contributions went directly into the pockets of the Sergeant and his associates.

Eventually, the pair picked upon a Sergeant Major in the Special Investigation Branch, who was a dedicated non-smoker and who had photographic evidence of the store men burning the holes. One by one, each store man confessed, divulging the names of his co-conspirators.

One thing led to another, and the Sergeant was Court Martialed and finished up in the military prison, where he still continued to run some inventive scams.

Desperate Manoeuvres

In November, it snowed so heavily that it lay thick upon the ground. It was then that our masters decided that the British army should undertake our first major military manoeuvre in arctic conditions. Our section was called upon to drive to a remote spot in the Black Forest and pitch our little open-ended tent in a clearing next to a forest crossroads.

I had with me the matchless 350 O.H.V. GL38 motorcycle, the suitability of which I was meant to be assessing for the British army.

We huddled together in our little tents, which we cunningly packed around with snow for greater insulation. The Black Forest was aptly named; it was a huge, menacing, shadowy forest, crisscrossed by paths of perfect white show and collapsed branches.

Our headquarters was set up in an ancient, long-deserted pigsty, and it was in its walls that our cook had set up a paraffin cooker and, together with his assistant, was very soon brewing up tea using melted snow, in which floated the occasional acorn. We ate tinned bacon, stew and beans and even twenty year old tinned chocolate. We ate snow, washed in snow, bathed in snow and even shaved in snow.

The first night we were there, in accordance with army customs, it was decided that we would all guard the camp in shifts of two hours a piece. My shift was due to take place at 2 o'clock in the morning, so I went to bed at 6p.m ... and slept until 10 o'clock the following morning.

I awoke to the birds singing and snow falling off branches — but otherwise, all was silence. I thought, "This is strange!"

I had slept straight through, and nobody had woken me. Why? I hopped round to the cooks' mess, still encased in my sleeping bag. To my astonishment, the camp was deserted. It turned out that my motorcycle, the one I was so proud of, had vanished, along with two army jeeps.

Apparently, my so-called comrades had taken it upon themselves to go for a drink or three, to which end they had taken the two jeeps some half a dozen miles along one of the tracks to a traditional Black Forest cafe.

It all boiled down to the fact that four of my friends (one Sergeant in charge and three corporals) were due to leave the army the following week, and they were suffering from a condition known as "demob happy", which induced them to take liberties that, under normal circumstances, they would never have done.

Anyway, as was quite normal with these communities, they were welcomed with open arms and were given large quantities of Schnapps, one of the most potent drinks known to man. It appears that a lot of friendly banter had arisen between the two parties, that is my friends and the German drinking population, over the merits of the German BMW motorcycle and the British Norton. It culminated in one of my inebriated friends driving back down to camp and loading my motorbike, which was not a known model in Germany, onto the back of the jeep and then demonstrating its versatility, presumably to win a bet. One of the Germans brought down his big old BMW, and they raced around the clearings, showing off, as was all too common with British troops.

By midnight, they were totally skint and well into their cups. Money had to come from somewhere to provide more Schnapps. And that's when the unthinkable happened. An old local farmer who had been admiring the bike, offered to buy it. At that time they had amassed a counter bill of nearly one hundred marks and, unfortunately, they had no money to pay. The motorcycle was worth considerably more than 100 marks, so the deal was done. They sold it for 120 marks — the 20 marks being my share.

Needless to say, there were some pretty sore heads by the time realisation dawned the next day. I was innocent, but I would have to bear the blame. To say that I was not happy would be putting it mildly. Our initial problem was that we did not know the name of the person who had bought the bike, though one of the café regulars was under the impression that his son worked in a factory about 20 miles away and that he had purchased the bike for his son to ride to work on.

We were in a real fix. If we had gone to the civilian police, I would have been Court Martialed for sure. Eventually, a plan was hatched, and we drove down to the nearest town, in which there were a dozen factories, and we hung around outside the factory gates.

Eventually, the son of the purchaser was seen to enter a factory gate on my motorcycle. We waited until late afternoon, then approached him. We offered him 120 marks for the motorcycle, which was what his father had paid for it. He refused point blank; he wanted at least 500 marks for it. This we had not got. He also threatened to go to the local newspaper. He had us over a barrel. A lot of telephone calls were made to sympathisers both in B.A.O.R. and the Depot, with a result of us raising 540 marks, which he accepted, and I rode the bike back to camp.

It was decided that it was too risky to have the bike outside Dusseldorf as it was attracting too much interest, and so I returned to Headquarters, and the duty driver took my place on the scheme.

The Arab

I was settling down to a quiet relaxing Saturday afternoon off, when the telephone rang — it was Q ringing up for transport. Q had a charmed life as a soldier, because every time something unpleasant materialised, such as manoeuvres in the snow, he claimed leave of absence on various pretexts, and while the rest of the Company was sweating or freezing, depending on the weather, he would be sitting nicely ensconced in a warm study, drinking lager and eating sausage and chips.

Under normal circumstances, his request would not have been a problem. Duty drivers rarely had to do anything more taxing at the weekend than pick up the occasional piece of mail or shoot down to the local wine merchants for a bottle of wine for the Officers' Mess. Even if I had to pick up a passenger on the pillion of the bike, providing I carried a spare helmet, there was no problem.

Anyway, Q rang to ask if I would collect him from the "Woes and Joes Club".

"Certainly Q; I'll be there in 10 minutes," I said.

The Woes and Joes Club occupied the top floor of the very modern *Presidium* (Police Station), which was a large imposing building rented to the British Army, and it presented one small problem which had totally slipped my mind. On the second floor were the medical offices of the police headquarters and on the fourth Saturday afternoon of the month, the ladies of the street were required by law to attend for medical examinations. I had the dubious pleasure of having to walk through them, being propositioned at least 100 times on the way. This may have seemed bad enough, but there was worse to come.

I duly presented myself at the Woes and Joes Club, and the Steward informed me that they had a large party there and as Q was in need of sobering, I was advised to wait.

While I sat waiting, the steward offered me a small plate of caviar and a glass of champagne, which I accepted. I cannot pretend that I enjoyed the caviar, in fact it tasted horrible, but I could not complain. Ten minutes later, and after what seemed like several trips to the lavatory, Q appeared. I could not believe my eyes — in place of Q was an Arab Sheik. He looked as if he had slept in the Arab costume for at least a week, and he stank of booze. He had been sick, and his clothes were in the laundry. I nearly had a fit when I realised that I was going to have to take him on the back of my motorbike in all his regalia. I did ask them if they had something to cover him, but they had nothing.

There he was, this man with an enormous paunch, hook nose and with a 5 o'clock shadow, waddling towards me. I couldn't decide whether to laugh or cry. Apparently, he had not been home for three or four days, which did not help. His wife was not happy, either.

I decided to try and sneak him down the back stairs and get him home as quickly as possible, as he only lived a mile away. I was trying not to arouse curiosity, but unfortunately I walked straight into a hoard of ladies of the street, who literally mobbed us as we came round the corner. My passenger was collecting cards as if there was no tomorrow. The next thing I knew, he had vanished into one of the lifts with a very large lady, leaving me standing like a fool, surrounded by women.

He finally reappeared with his turban disarrayed, so that it kept hanging over his face like a pair of curtains. He was more unsteady than ever. I escaped the clutches of the ladies, but not without losing my armband and half my tie. I was also covered in lipstick. I finally managed to get the great fool out to the rear courtyard, where the bike stood.

After several false starts, I managed to get him seated upon the pillion of the bike and finally, having been push-started by scores of high heeled young ladies, and with him standing up on the back foot rests, swearing undying love and blowing kisses to the cheering mob, we were on our way. He continued to wave and call after every pretty girl he saw; frequently leaning over so far that we were in imminent danger of crashing. Every time I had to turn the bike to go right, instead of leaning his body into the angle of our ride, he resolutely balanced his body the opposite way, so that the bike steered an erratic course between kerb stones.

I toiled down the street at the awe-inspiring speed of ten miles an hour. Unfortunately we caught the attention of all the kids in the area who were doing cartwheels for tourists. Many of them reached up to touch him, and the silly fool pushed money into their grasping little hands.

"Just another hundred yards," I thought, "and this nightmare will be over."

The block of high-rise apartments in which he lived was just around the corner. "Just a few more yards, and I can drop him off, then I'm home and free."

Was I heck!

At that moment, the large staff car of the Provost Marshall himself pulled up alongside us. I groaned inwardly. I had already escaped one Court Martial that week, now it looked as though I was in danger of another one.

The driver wound down his window.

"Compliments of the Colonel, he would like a word."

I managed to get my passenger off the motorbike, and he stood and swayed, while I went around to the back door of the Colonel's compartment, aware that I was covered in lipstick, armband gone and what remained of my tie half way round my collar. I saluted him as smartly as I could.

"What's this man?" asked the Colonel. "Are you some circus freak show?"

I thought hard. Meanwhile, Q was still handing out money to the kids and swaying gently.

"Who is this individual?" he demanded "And what's he doing on your bike?"

I lied desperately. "I was ordered to pick him up sir. I understand that he is an Arab delegate at the Conference (there was a big peace conference going on in the town) and his transport has let him down."

The Colonel looked at me suspiciously. "Umph!"

The next moment he addressed Q in what I believe was Arabic.

Oh my goodness, I thought, that's torn it. Then miracle of miracles, Q answered in the same language like a native born. You could have knocked me down with a feather. They chatted for a minute or two in Arabic, and then the Colonel got out and bravely saluted Q and shook his hand.

"Well done," he said to me, and then he was gone.

I felt weak at the knees. We had just a few yards to go, and then we were at the front gate of his married quarters.

He seemed to sober up rather suddenly, and I soon found out why. We staggered drunkenly up the garden path, falling into the flowerbed just the once. Suddenly the front door flew open with a crash, and there stood the lady of the house.

Q insisted that I come inside. Meanwhile, his other half hovered around like a small, black thundercloud.

For 2 hours I was stuck there, during which time I learned that Q had been in the Palestine Police before transferring to the British Military Police — hence his expertise in Arabic. Having been forced to look through photographs of Q in his Palestine Uniform, I eventually managed to make my escape, and, as I tiptoed over the doormat, I heard the first sounds of shattering crockery.

Anti-Vice Squad

In the last half of my second year, about October, I was promoted to the Head of the Anti-vice Liaison in B.A.O.R. 4. It sounded great — however it was not all that it was cracked up to be. The Anti-Vice Squad consisted of one person — me — plus the services of a part-time interpreter. I spent most of the time running around on my motorbike, chasing forms. What sort of forms you might ask? These were questionnaires supplied by the Local V.D. Hospital and filled in by soldiers who had been infected by local prostitutes.

It was my job to interview these soldiers; the idea being that we could identify the ladies who had given the soldiers the infection, then report them to the German Police Vice Squad, who would insist that they have a medical examination, with the hope that they could be cured.

The problem was that, even if we found them, it was purely voluntary on the part of the ladies concerned whether they had treatment or not. Quite a few refused treatment, and all we could do was to warn the local soldiers.

The forms also presented a problem, as they were filled in by infected soldiers who had invariably been drunk and so could only recall sketchy details of the episode. A good clear description, as far as we were concerned, was that she was a woman in a red dress called Matilda. She was short and fat, sometimes tall and thin, and aged between 15 and 75. This description applied inevitably to the same woman who had infected a dozen soldiers in the one evening. It was a well known fact that the Russian side was sending these ladies down into the west to infect as many soldiers as possible, and I have no doubt that the Americans were doing exactly the same thing on the other side. (Thank goodness it was not AIDS at that time, or half the population would have died.)

It was a thankless, boring job. I trucked around the countryside on a motorcycle with these forms, staying at various camps overnight as the fancy took me.

There was not a large variety of drugs about, *but there was* a little heroin and a lot of cannabis. The cannabis was a pretty bad one as it caused an awful lot of paranoia. I once saw a woman throw herself through a plate glass window under the influence of this drug. It was also the cause of a lot of fights, especially when combined with beer. Once addicts were hooked on it, they were really hooked. Most of the drugs came in from Holland, and the drug gangs seemed to have control of everything; Amsterdam was the most notorious hot spot. We did the occasional raid, but it was pretty obvious that we were trying to tackle a mountain with a tablespoon.

My most abiding memory of being on the Vice Squad was walking with a female German officer across a large plain of demolished buildings at the rear of

Dusseldorf city centre. In the middle of it was a large set of steps leading down into a complex of cellars in which were a series of furnished rooms, occupied by prostitutes. The people used to call it "The Warren".

The officer and I sat in a waiting room like a pair of lemons, waiting to interview a woman, whilst men were dodging about all over the place, trying to avoid us. I think we ruined that afternoon's trade.

There is, however, a more pleasant memory of that period. Christmas Eve — the last Christmas I had in the forces, when everybody in the Company who was able to go, were taken to a big burnt-out cathedral, which was minus its roof, together with hundreds of German civilians. There, we listened to a glorious choral thanksgiving, whilst the snow swirled down through the open roof.

All too soon it was time to go back to Civvy Street. My two years' National Service almost up, we went back on the troop train into Holland, and then took the boat to Harwich, U.K. Another train took us to Woking, Surrey and Inkerman Barracks. When we reached the depot, we were prepared to be demobbed.

We were there for two days. On the last day, representatives of police forces around the country came and tried to recruit us into various civilian police forces. I myself took a chance and was recruited into the police force in Oxfordshire.

I had to go to Aylesbury to be demobbed, which meant going on the train from Woking to the Territorial Centre, where I had to give in my cap, belt, flashes and badges. The basic uniform I was allowed to keep, otherwise I would have gone home naked. They gave me a beret and badge saying "Queens Own Oxfordshire Hussars", and then I was put on a bus and taken all the way home to Oxford — a journey of about an hour and a half.

My dad was delighted to see me, so was my mother. My brothers and sisters, however, couldn't have cared less. Then my dad came up with something special, a homecoming present. While I had been in the army, I had been sending home £1 per week, which was quite a lot when you consider that I was only getting 30 shillings a week. Instead of spending it, he had saved it and bought me a motorbike. It was a B.S.A. Bantom 125 cc 2 stroke — not new, but in extremely good condition. It was my pride and joy! I was so grateful to my father because when I came out of the army, apart from a few shillings, I was skint. I was now mobile.

I had six weeks to wait until I could take a job, so I wandered around the countryside, enjoying my new toy. One glorious morning, I found myself heading towards the home of the Misses Franklin.

I arrived at the long drive of the Franklins' farm with its white-painted picket fence. The horses, now very fat, were romping in the hay meadow, and I stopped the engine for a few moments to admire the view and to listen in silence to the sound of larks, wood pigeons and, from the green and gold of the Cumner Hills, the first call of the cuckoo. The river ran past the bottom of the drive, a light bluish flash across the landscape. The cottage stood, picturesque, on the bank, and Bert's little motorboat was tied up to the old willow tree. Bert himself was digging in his front garden.

The great grey tractors were crawling around the main farm house, dragging all sorts of implements around the fields. I could see two housemaids cleaning the windows and a third pegging out clothes.

I caught the flash of green and blue Kingfishers diving for fish in the slow running stream, and a little further on, two majestic swans chivvying a small family of indignant ducks.

Could this be paradise, I thought to myself?

I saw Susan Franklin come out onto the front steps of the large house and, on seeing me, came towards me with delighted cries of welcome. Taking me by the hand, she led me into the big kitchen, where Henry Smith and Bert, who had by that time gone into the house, were busy with the kitchen sink, obviously re-plumbing it.

Moments later, Annette came into the kitchen and gave me a hug. I noticed a strange thing about Henry — he had totally lost his foreign accent, and he spoke with the local burr. Bert, of course, was still the same. It had transpired that he had married his lady love and was now living in his cottage upon the banks of the river.

We sat around the big table drinking coffee and tea, the others bringing me up to speed with all the things that had been happening whilst I had been away.

I asked Susan what had happened to the travellers. Apparently, the old lady still lived in the house, where

148

she had been nursed back to health, and the estate had employed the son.

"What about the strange language?" I asked.

"Oh, that was quite simple," replied Susan. "The poor dear could only speak Welsh."

She explained what had happened. The lady's husband originally came from the North Pembrokeshire area, where he was a railway man. At the beginning of the war, he had been transferred to London. They kept themselves to themselves and only spoke Welsh within the family, as she was not able to converse in English. Her son, who had a cleft pallet, could converse in English, but it was impossible for him to be understood.

When their house was totally destroyed by a V2 Rocket, the husband had been killed, and the old lady was placed in a nursing home, where she was unable to get anyone to understand her. Consequently, she was ignored by the staff there.

Her son had been placed in the YMCA, where he was bullied. Eventually, he managed to trace his mother, and they decided that he should go to a specialist unit to learn a trade. He'd also had an operation for his cleft pallet and was now making himself understood.

Although they were still there, they really wanted to go home to their roots.

Mrs Beppo, (who we met in a previous book) the lovely Italian, Welsh speaking lady, had become very friendly with the Franklin sisters, and it was she who pointed out to the others that their guest could only speak Welsh. She therefore acted as interpreter.

"So what about Gethsemene?" I asked. "What did that mean?"

"Simple — it is a little hamlet above Fishguard, where they were born. They still have an old cottage near the cliff path there that has been empty for many years. Seeing you has given me an idea. For some time we have been planning a trek up the A40 to take the old lady and her son back home. How would you like to come with us? We would pay you well, and you would be the courier for our little party. Bert has built not one, but three magnificent caravans, each one pulled by two Shire horses. We shall also take one of the tractors with a long cart, upon which we shall be carrying our tents and chairs. What do you say?"

"I say — Great!" I said.

We celebrated with a drop of sherry and shook hands.

Susan said, "Here's to the good companions!"

Excited as I was, I just knew that it would be an eventful journey.

Also available in ISIS Large Print:

Return to Wigan Pier

Ted Dakin

"One Saturday night when the alehouse was busy, we hopped over the yard wall, gathered a few pop bottles from the bottom crates and over the next few days handed them back to an unsuspecting landlord for money."

Ted Dakin's third memoir is filled with more tales of his childhood in Wigan. In *Return to Wigan Pier* Ted also compares today's weather with winters past, housing then and now, gambling habits, the recession and even the habit of Church goers. On a more personal note Ted also shares tales of games of spin the bottle and grief in the community, which led to wrestling lessons in the name of helping a close friend.

ISBN 978-0-7531-5269-0 (hb)
ISBN 978-0-7531-5270-6 (pb)

We Waved to the Baker

Andrew Arbuckle

"I wished I had asked Mum to buy my most recent favourite food, a raisin-filled slice of cake that the baker called a 'fly cemetery'. This was rather a strange name because I never saw any dead flies when I was eating it."

We Waved to the Baker is an evocative and heart-warming collection of stories from Andrew Arbuckle's youth in Fife. Through the fresh gaze of childhood, he depicts the rugged hard work of life on the farm, while capturing the essence of growing up in a boisterous family and close rural community. We follow the young Andrew as he deals with the trials and tribulations of school, older brothers and plucking chickens, while throwing in as much mischief as possible.

ISBN 978-0-7531-9590-1 (hb)
ISBN 978-0-7531-9591-8 (pb)

Bitter Fruit

Rod Broome

The first twelve months of my career proved to be highly eventful. I was appointed to teach at a junior school . . . succumbed to a nasty dose of pneumonia caused — everyone said — by living in a cold, damp, rented flat; and on Christmas Eve I became engaged to Anita, the most wonderful girl in the world!

In the final part of the "Broome" Trilogy, Rod Broome describes his early days in teaching; a head teacher who died in post, his first position as head teacher in a new open-plan primary school and how this caused staff to learn new methods of teaching. He recalls the day the school got its first computer, and the afternoon when the caretaker dressed up as a snowman!

ISBN 978-0-7531-9582-6 (hb)
ISBN 978-0-7531-9583-3 (pb)

Wicksy and the Concert Party

Peter Wicks

"In many ways, certainly for the first couple of years, I was to find that I was a square peg in a round hole."

Peter Wicks returns to tell his hilarious tales of being a teenager. Having been awarded a scholarship Peter attended Southfield Grammar school in Oxford alongside fee paying students who at times endeavoured to make school life difficult for young Wicksy. Peter remembers vividly each school building, its every twist and turn and the personalities of the teachers who brought it to life.

Early days at the school were a struggle for Peter but when he makes a drastic decision and his pet dog Pat bounds defiantly after him, he learns how life can take an unexpected turn for the better and begins to push himself to the top of the class.

ISBN 978-0-7531-8378-6 (hb)
ISBN 978-0-7531-8379-3 (pb)

Wicksy

Peter Wicks

"On my fourth birthday, I was presented with a beautifully made, yellow painted, pedal car. I remember that it had a horn, battery operated lights and a proper hand brake. I grew so attached to that car that I insisted upon having all my meals in it."

Brought up in and around Oxford, Peter Wicks brings his memoirs to life with a riot of colourful stories. From picnics with his parents via school days and bullies to spending summer holidays with his grandmother, Wicksy's tales are a charming look at a wartime childhood.

He also touches on the difficulties faced at the time, with air raid sirens, gas masks and wartime shortages, and the sad death of a childhood friend.

ISBN 978-0-7531-9502-4 (hb)
ISBN 978-0-7531-9503-1 (pb)

ISIS publish a wide range of books in large print, from fiction to biography. Any suggestions for books you would like to see in large print or audio are always welcome. Please send to the Editorial Department at:

ISIS Publishing Limited
7 Centremead
Osney Mead
Oxford OX2 0ES

A full list of titles is available free of charge from:

Ulverscroft Large Print Books Limited

(UK)
The Green
Bradgate Road, Anstey
Leicester LE7 7FU
Tel: (0116) 236 4325

(Australia)
P.O. Box 314
St Leonards
NSW 1590
Tel: (02) 9436 2622

(USA)
P.O. Box 1230
West Seneca
N.Y. 14224-1230
Tel: (716) 674 4270

(Canada)
P.O. Box 80038
Burlington
Ontario L7L 6B1
Tel: (905) 637 8734

(New Zealand)
P.O. Box 456
Feilding
Tel: (06) 323 6828

Details of **ISIS** complete and unabridged audio books are also available from these offices. Alternatively, contact your local library for details of their collection of **ISIS** large print and unabridged audio books.